In Search Of The Diamond Brooch

A Southern Family's Account of 1820s Pioneer
Florida Through The Civil War to Modern Day

Written by:
Terri Gerrell
Pete Gerrell

Compiled by: Terri Gerrell

SYP Publishing
Tallahassee, Fl

Southern Yellow Pine
Publishing

Published by
Southern Yellow Pine (SYP) Publishing
4351 Natural Bridge Rd.
Tallahassee, FL 32305

www.syppublishing.com
The contents and opinions expressed in this book do not necessarily reflect the views and opinions of Southern Yellow Pine Publishing, nor does the mention of brands or trade names constitute endorsement.

ISBN-10: 0985706201

ISBN-13: 978-0-9857062-0-3

Printed in the United States of America
First Edition
September 2012

DEDICATION

I'm putting this book together in memory of my husband. Allen R. "Pete" Gerrell. Throughout our life together, he stood beside me and made me stronger in every way. He encouraged me to be more than I was and to try new and different things.

He was forever exposing me to and thrusting me into something new I had never thought to dream of, yet alone experience. It would seem that this is one more such item. Pete started this project before his death in 2007. It needed to be finished for him and the generations to come.

This would not be complete without mentioning my grandchildren. These stories and the history included are for you.

CONTENTS

ACKNOWLEDGEMENTS

I need to mention here my fiancé Charles Turner. He inspired me to pick this up and finally put it together. I'm not sure he knew what he was getting into but I need to thank him for all the patience, love, and understanding when I was up late at night writing or buried in research.

I want to acknowledge Jessica Barnett and Marilee Gerrell Butler who graciously allowed portions of their work to be reprinted here. Thanks also go to Holly Gerrell who offered much needed technical advice.

I have to include one more group of people here and that is the members of the Gerrell family who helped me find pictures and other details. I thank you for the time you took answering my questions, telling me your stories and all the other little things that came up.

INTRODUCTION TG

Pete's favorite method of discussing history was The 3 Rs Method; Rambling, Reminiscing and Repeating. He also wrote history that way. <u>In Search of The Diamond Brooch</u> was the first book he started. His historical interests were so vast that he rambled through and completed two other books. He was working on this one and a fourth at the time of his death. Since some of this book is based on his previously unpublished writings, I will also be using his methodology. Some of this includes research on Leon and Wakulla County. It also includes a history of the Gerrell family and their ancestors. Portions of the book written by Pete Gerrell will be so indicated with a PG. Those written by Terri Gerrell will be indicated with a TG.

The Gerrell family has its Florida roots in the early 1800s. The first branch of the family to settle here was the Halls. The original land owned in 1827 is still in the family. Pete was a sixth generation Floridian. His grandchildren can claim to be eighth generation. It is unusual for a family to remain so stationary for so many generations in this country. As a result of this, the family history is well documented with artifacts and documents. It also has its share of stories and legends that have been passed through the generations. I will try to include both here.

By including both I also risk not having everyone agree with me. If you ever played telephone when you were a child at a party and passed a message around the room, you know that the message could sometimes get distorted. You also know that those messages still had some truth in them. I am documenting stories, some of which have been passed down for generations. They may well have been distorted. So you ask, why include them at all?

I included them because I am of the belief that folklore and telling our stories is just as important as documented facts. Where there are facts that match up, I will try to point that out. What I do know is that with each successive generation we lose a bit more of our history and our family lore. For this reason, I am writing down and documenting what I can. I want my grandsons and their children to be able to read about their family. I hope this preserves a little of what might otherwise have washed away with time.

CHAPTER ONE

ELIZABETH BYRD HALL - TG

This story needs to start with the first ancestor to settle in North Florida. Elizabeth Byrd Hall came to Wakulla County from North Carolina after the death of her husband, Enoch Hall. Family lore states she wanted to be closer to her younger brother Benjamin Byrd. They were direct descendents of William Byrd, founder of Richmond, VA. Her husband died in 1825. We believe she arrived around 1827.

She arrived, imagine this, with her children and six Negro slaves along with her wagons of household goods. That would have taken guts, strength and stamina to move away from a civilized area to go to the wilderness as a widow. She established a home in the woods east of the St. Marks River. Her brother Benjamin Byrd was a merchant in the town of Magnolia on the west edge of the St. Marks River. He was also postmaster and a councilman for the city. Elizabeth and her family settled on land about a mile from Magnolia. She had an 80 acre land grant on the east side of the St. Marks River, north of Magnolia. Elizabeth raised her family in the area and added to her land holdings in the Newport census district. In 1860, the Newport census district was the fifth largest in Florida. The people were located along the river between St. Marks and the county line just south of Natural Bridge. Fewer people settled to the west because of the Forbes Purchase. Carving a home out of the unsettled North Florida wilderness would have been difficult to say the least.

Her children were Hiram, Lewis, Ahijah, Enoch, Elijah, Mahala, & Mary. Hiram moved back to Georgia. The others stayed in the area. Ahijah Hall was one of the first sheriffs in the county from 1845-1853. Family stories claim him as the first sheriff. I am not sure of that; my research indicates he may have been the second. Ahijah was very active in county politics and activities. He owned land in the area now known as Wakulla Station. It was known as Oil Still Station at the time. He built and ran a turpentine fire still there close to the St. Marks Railroad. His holdings in the turpentine business were sold to Newton Culbreath who formed the Wakulla Turpentine Company that operated until the end of the industry. In 1866, Ahijah was one of six people named by the Florida Legislature to act as a Commissioner to permanently choose a location for the county site of Wakulla. (General Assembly of Florida, Dec. 18, 1865)

Various members of the family were active in Magnolia and Wakulla County. Elizabeth's son Lewis Hall married Sarah Faircloth. They had seven children. One of their children was Lewis Franklin, our direct ancestor. Lewis and his son Lewis Franklin Hall were blacksmiths, farmers, gunsmiths and coopers. They were resourceful in doing everything they needed to do to provide for their families. Mary married John Coleman who I will mention later. Elijah was listed as a farmer in the 1860 Census.

Elizabeth later remarried a man by the name of Aaron Johnson in 1835. It is believed he was a farmer as a younger man. In the 1850s he was working for the Georgia-Florida Plank Road Company. He built a home at the intersections of the Tallahassee and Chaires branch of the road at Johnson Springs, later known as Rhodes Springs. He was the keeper of the Plank Road toll station until it closed in the late 1850s. The Plank Road's demise was caused by the reconstruction and conversion of the Tallahassee - St. Marks Railroad to steel rails and steam locomotive power.

Lewis Franklin was also a gunsmith during the time guns were being changed from flintlocks to cap and ball. We know where the home site was. A photo follows later in this chapter. The memories of Jessie French Gerrell and Frankie French Blackburn have allowed us to identify outbuildings such as the barn and the buildings used for blacksmithing and gun repair. We have found many artifacts at this site including farm tools and hundreds of antique gun parts.

Lewis Franklin married Mary Jane Moore On August 27, 1867 shortly after the Civil War. They had known each other all their lives. At the time Mary Jane was a widow. She had previously been married to Matthew Burns, a Civil War veteran, who died just after the war. He was 23 at the time. She already had two children from her first marriage. All the families had been neighbors and friends.

2

When Mary Jane was a little girl she was responsible for the title of this book.

IN SEARCH OF THE DIAMOND BROOCH   <u>TG</u>

Pete Gerrell was fond of saying, "I've spent my life in search of a diamond brooch." When he said that, he was referring to the favorite family story about little Mary Jane Moore. Our home is full of artifacts excavated from various pioneer home sites. People would frequently ask Pete what in the world inspired him to go around digging up all this stuff. This story was told to Pete when he was just a young child. The story inflamed a young boy's imagination and fanned a love of history and family.

Pete's Great Grandmother, Mary Jane Moore, was a young child of perhaps 4 or 5. When she grew up she married Lewis Franklin Hall who was Elizabeth Hall's grandson. For this story, she was young enough that she played with dolls frequently and had limited communication skills, perhaps 3-5 years of age.

The Moores were neighbors living just down The Pinhook Road. There was a death and thus a funeral where the families were together. Mary Jane Moore went to the funeral with her family. At the funeral, which was open casket, she observed the deceased woman dressed in all her finery with a brooch pinned to her dress. The funeral proceeded and the woman was buried. The mourners went home and returned to their daily lives.

A few days later, great-great-Grandma Sarah Faircloth Hall, noticed a piece of jewelry, her diamond brooch, was missing. A search began. With questioning, Mary Jane admitted she borrowed the brooch to play with. She dressed her favorite doll and pinned the brooch to her and had a funeral. She told the family she buried the doll. The problem was she was not sure where she buried it. It might have been around the yard or, it might have been out there in the corn field. The family searched high and low. It is said they even dug up part of the nearby corn field. In the days of plowing with a mule, this was not done lightly. As the story goes, neither the brooch nor the doll was ever seen again. Little Mary Jane was just not sure where she buried that doll baby.

And thus, Pete Gerrell spent his life "in search of the diamond brooch" digging for family history and family artifacts!

3

Mary Jane Moore Hall 1842-1908

MaryJane and Lewis Franklin had five children. They both lived long lives. Family legend states that Lewis Franklin did not believe in slavery. He did fight in the Civil War; however this was probably more about protecting his home and economic issues rather than the issue of slavery. After the war, a black man by the name of Rube Nick came to him. He had been a slave of another family member, Ahijah. Rube asked for a place to stay and for work. Lewis Franklin agreed. Rube worked for him until his death. He is the only black buried in the cemetery whose name we know. Rube Nick is buried on the far south of the cemetery. His stone states, former slave, 1816-1875. There are others there but, sadly their names have been lost.

As mentioned, this family has been in this area for a very long time. Another part of life is death. It was necessary to have a cemetery.

There was a hill nearby that was chosen for the family cemetery. It is The Hall Place Cemetery and it is still owned and maintained by the family. In the past it was used by many of the area families. Several old surnames in Wakulla & Leon County history can be found buried here i.e., Moores, Hamlin's, Duggars, Halls, Frenches, Colemans, Vickers etc. The site is still being used by the family. There are graves from the 1800's until the present. There are soldiers from many of our country's conflicts buried there. We have lost a view of the names over the years but have since recorded all we know so we do not lose anymore.

The newest grave is Pete Gerrell, my husband who wrote: The Illustrated History of the Naval Stores, Old Trees, and portions of this book. He is buried by a fat lightered tree stump that was a cat face in the turpentine woods. His tomb stone is a piece of marble from the Old Florida State Capital. He was involved in the redo many years ago. When they took the old marble to the dump he salvaged a piece. He was always very pleased with it but could never decide what to do with it. At his death I decided there was no better use than to memorialize him.

Here is an example of historic rambling. The story of Lewis Franklin Hall took us to the cemetery. Now we return to his family. In later years after his death, his home went to his daughter Grace Hall Alexander and her husband Amos Alexander. There will be more stories about Lewis and Mary Jane in the Civil War chapters.

The Alexander's lived at the Hall Place home site for several years. Amos was a farmer and general laborer according to the 1910 census. (United States Government, 1910) The family is listed as living in Pinhook, Florida. Their first child, Wright Alexander was born while living there and is shown in his mother's arms in the photo of the Hall Place site. They had eight children.

Amos was known to family members as Uncle Pig. It is said he liked to play cards and gamble a little. He had a table under a shade tree in front of the house where he would gather with his friends. The old live oak tree in the photo is still on the property which has allowed us to know the exact location of the house. Several wedding bands and loose coins were found in the vicinity of the table. Amos died fairly young in 1939. His wife, Aunt Grace, lived until 1974. (Butler, 1996) Many of the Alexanders' in Wakulla County today are descendents of this couple.

Lewis Franklin Hall

Hall Home Site c.1905

Pictured are Grace Hall Alexander and her husband Amos Alexander with infant Wright Alexander Sr.

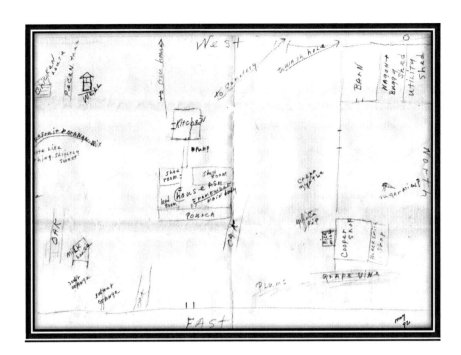

1992 Drawing by Frank French Burns of

Hall Home Site Lay Out.

Gun Parts From Lewis Hall Home Site

I've spent a fair amount of time talking about the Halls. However, there is another side to this family. The Halls led to the Frenches. Jessie French Married Walter Gerrell. There were no male heirs of Jim French. Thus, the Frenches became Gerrells. Jessie French married Walter Gerrell in 1930.

The Gerrell name also has a long history in this area. And as with the other side of the family, the name was not originally Gerrell. So we have a lot of local family names but, none of them are Gerrell. How did that happen?

Once again, let us imagine and travel back to the 1850s.

All lines of the family were in the area between 1825 and 1850. All lines were also involved in an industry or occupation that depended on the land, the forest, and by default turpentine.

John Daniel Wiggins settled in an area known as Hickory Grove in 1825. This area was south of present day Woodville about ten miles south of the Florida Capitol Building. This land was where the Tallahassee Railroad Company's new railroad was planned to go. John knew of the threat of the Seminole Indians and chose this location because of its proximity to Fort Stansbury, a United States Indian War Fort. It was just a few miles northeast of Wakulla Springs. John had been a farmer in South Carolina before moving to Florida. He thought this new land would surely be good enough farm land to support his family and livestock. As it turned out, the dry sandy soil he first cleared was worn out within a few short years. Soil in this area is still difficult to farm without good fertilization. He had to continuously clear new ground.

It was fortunate for the Wiggins family that Florida's First Territorial Governor, Richard Keith Call, was planning Florida's first railroad. The railroad would connect Tallahassee to St. Marks. It was to become North Central Florida's only outlet to the north and other areas. A railroad from Jacksonville was completed years later.

All of the heart pine materials that the rails, sleepers, and ties were built of had to be cut and hand hewn in the nearby woods. The Wiggins became involved in supplying these materials and transporting them by ox team to the road site. There was no shortage of wood materials. The forest floor was literally covered with heart pine (fat lighter) logs. Until this time they had only been used to build split rail fences and the nearby fort.

It took three attempts and seven years time to get a charter for the railroad approved. After this, construction began on the railroad. The railroad was placed into service in November 1837. The need for hand hewn wood materials continued. Originally the railroad was wood timbers. The cars were pulled by mules or oxen. Later the railroad was improved to steel rails with a steam locomotive engine. This changed and revolutionized the area.

George Edward Gerrell, Pete's great-grandfather, came to the St. Marks River with his wife Margaret Morris Gerrell in about 1850. George Edward was a cooper by trade, specializing in tight cooperage. From the few remaining available records; it is evident that he bought several tracts of land with white oak and hickory. The first tract was a hammock bordering the west side of the St. Marks River immediately north of the town of Magnolia. When George Edward and his employees worked out of timber on these forty or more acres, they moved north and bought at least two more tracts before being interrupted by the Civil War. George Edward joined Gamble's Artillery of Jefferson County in 1862. He later transferred to Jerry Kilcrease's Company on May 27, 1863. (Allen R. Gerrell, 1993). In March 1865, he was at home on wounded leave; however, he rejoined his unit at Newport and helped stop the Union troops at Natural Bridge.

George Edward Gerrell was never able to recover his cooperage business after the war. He died of his war wounds in the mid 1870s.

Well now, we have Gerrells, but they needed a wife, or family, to continue. So now we talk about the Castillo's. Shortly after the Tallahassee - St. Marks Railroad opened the north central Florida frontier to the outside world, two brothers of Castilian Spanish descent sailed into St. Marks from Tampa Bay. The Castillo brothers set up a sailing fleet for transporting supplies into and out of St. Marks. They came to this area from Tampa because they knew the railroad was being built and this would bring profitable business to the coast for their trade goods.

John and Antonio Castillo were Spanish mariners. They needed pitch or pine tar for sealing the wooden boats and treating the sailing ropes. Wood ships in those days did not function without pine,

9

turpentine, or naval stores products. While searching for a supply of pitch, they traveled north along the railroad into the virgin pine forest. About eight miles up the track, they met the Wiggins family.

The Wiggins' had previously built tar kilns in South Carolina and knew how to produce pitch. The two families soon reached an agreement and the Wiggins' began producing pitch for the sailing vessels in St. Marks. As a result of family interactions and meetings, John Jesse Wiggins and Isabella Castillo were soon married. These were Pete Gerrell's paternal great grandparents

Minnie Lee Wiggins was a descendent of this group. She married George Alan Gerrell in 1892. George was very tall and thin. He was known for being a quiet man. His grandchildren remember looking way up at him. He was a hard working Woodville farmer. His wife was a busy vibrant lady as a young woman. She was also quite a business woman. She had multiple profitable real estate dealings through the years. The couple had settled on farmland three miles east of Woodville just south of what is now Natural Bridge Rd. They had seven children. The children were Ira, William Everett, James Castello, Walter D., Margaret, Allie, and Doris Isabelle.

Walter D. Gerrell did many things throughout his life. He worked as a butcher and a farmer when young. Later he was involved in the timber industry, including dead head logging. He was also involved in land sales and early development of the Woodville area. He was the son of George Alan Gerrell and Minnie Lee Wiggins. He married Jessie French in 1930.

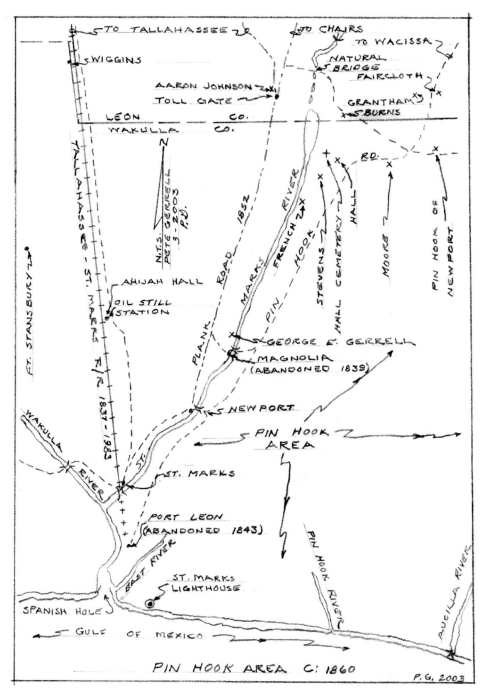

1860 Pinhook Area Map

With Home sites & Major Landmarks

Farm & Blacksmith Tools Found
At Hall Place Home Site

CHAPTER TWO

THE BATTLE OF NATURAL BRIDGE; TALLAHASSEE <u>TG</u>

Family Stories from the Battle of Natural Bridge

During March of 1865, the civil war was drawing to a close, however in some parts of the country there was a still a lot of activity. Here in Florida the Union was busy trying to get into Tallahassee. Tallahassee was the only southern capital not taken during the war. The Union landed soldiers along the Florida coast. It was decided to march up the east side of the St Marks River to try to approach Tallahassee. First they came through Newport. There was a battle or skirmish there and they proceeded up the river. Once past Newport they were marching through territory that belonged to some of the Gerrell ancestors and neighbors. The land belonged to people with the names of Hall, Stevens, French, & Burns to name a few. It is helpful to know a little of the history to appreciate how the family stories fit in.

So first; a brief history of the battle as researched and written by Marilee Gerrell Butler (Butler, 1996).There is also a general map so you can see the picture in your mind.

THE BATTLE OF NATURAL BRIDGE by: Marilee G. Butler

"Lest We Forget"

One of this writer's first and best memories is going "over the river" to Granddaddy French's house. Seeing the eagle high atop the Confederate monument at Natural Bridge was always an exciting high-light of the trip. The memories that we have of "over the river" (and they are many and precious) must necessarily include the Natural Bridge and its history, which we came to love as we grew older.

Because our ancestor, Lewis Franklin Hall, was involved in the

Battle of Natural Bridge in an unusual way, and because the Union forces were fighting on the ground that our Granddaddy Jim French would one day many years later place his RFD mailbox on, we descendants of these Halls and Frenches have a special interest in this place, Natural Bridge.

Photo of the Florida State Capitol with The Confederate Flag. Courtesy of the Florida Photographic Collection; State Archives of Florida, Florida Memory, http://floridamemory.com/items/show/43426

Many years later, in 1922, Granddaddy Jim French and our Grandmother Mollie would give to The United Daughters of the Confederacy two acres of land for a memorial to the brave Confederates who fought here. The Rhodes family also gave an additional four acres of land. The Anna Jackson Chapter of the UDC gave these six acres to the State of Florida for the purpose of "establishing a park and erecting a monument at the scene of the Battle of Natural Bridge". This six acres is now Natural Bridge State Park.

The War was winding down to its bitter conclusion in March of 1865 when Union forces (mostly Negro troops) under the leadership of Brig. General John Newton came ashore near the St. Marks Lighthouse with the intention of capturing St. Marks and Tallahassee. This operation had originated in Key West and had included two black regiments, the Second and the Ninety-Ninth United States Colored Troops, and the Second Florida (Union) Cavalry.

Lieut. Colonel George Washington Scott was commanding the Fifth Florida Cavalry Battalion and had skirmished with the Federal troops as they moved inland from the coast. Scott's troops were gradually falling back toward Newport.

Sue M. Archer was a student at the female department of West Florida Seminary and sister of one of the cadets who went to Natural Bridge. She related that on Saturday March 4 the shrill whistle of a train was heard late in the evening, an unusual hour for a train to come in. A special engine had been sent to Tallahassee from St. Marks to alert the town that the Yankees had landed.

Troops were called out from every available source. William Milton's Company from Marianna, Cap't. Joseph Dunham commanding, Col. Love's Militia, the local militia/reserves, troops from Madison and many other places in Middle, East, and West Florida came.

A group of old citizens from Gadsden County called "the Gadsden Grays" came along to fight. Dr. Charles Hentz called these men "the Silver Grays, all of the old citizens of Quincy, and the adjacent county". None was under 50 years of age.

Governor Milton ordered out the cadets from West Florida Seminary in Tallahassee mere boys in age from 14 to 18, about forty-five in number (some sources say twenty-six). These young cadets called out to battle would later be called "the Baby Corps". West Florida Seminary in later years would become Florida State University. Because of the cadets' participation in the Battle of Natural Bridge, Florida State University flies the Battle streamer which was awarded to the ROTC corps in 1957, " ..... to be affixed to the staffs of the flags which bear the seal of the University, a streamer which bears the words NATURAL

BRIDGE 1865". This is one of only three such decorations awarded, the other two going to Virginia Military Institute for the Battle of New Market and to the Citadel for its actions at Ft. Sumter.

The enemy, arriving at Newport, found that they could not cross the St. Marks River there because Confederate troops had burned the bridge over the river and were ready to repulse the enemy.

The battle at Newport took place on Sunday afternoon and the town was shelled by the Yankees. "Women and children had to fly to the forest to save their lives", wrote Gus West in Battle of Natural Bridge 1919. "My mother, with her baby girl in her arms and her little boy found safety in flight."

John R Blocker in the Tallahassee Daily Democrat 1918 wrote, "we gave them (the enemy) a warm reception for about an hour" (at Newport).

Union leaders decided to head for Natural Bridge in Leon County- the next available crossing of the river. It was a distance of some eight miles north of Newport and they traveled on "an old and unfrequented road" on the east side of the river.

"The sun came up gloriously", one writer said of the morning of March 6. Confederate troops had begun arriving at Natural Bridge before dawn-the young cadets from Tallahassee and the "Gadsden-Grays" from Quincy among them. Colonel Scott and his men came up the Plank Road from Newport on the west side of the river along with other troops. They waited in the Monday dawn of March 6, a semi-circle of muskets and artillery behind earthen mounds that are still visible today.

By 11:00 A.M. the enemy was there in full force and opened fire with its artillery. James Phineas Wilson wrote "The entire line of our Entrenchments were nearly one-half mile in length, well-occupied by veterans but chiefly by Reserve and Militia Infantry and Artillery. (My ancestor, George Edward Gerrell, was there with Kilcrease Battery, one of the artillery units at the battle. M.G.B.) Our artillery consisted of seven cannons. The firing was now rapid and continuous, and four separate efforts were made to pass through the narrow defile formed by the rising and sinking of the river. The Natural Bridge was a place where the St. Marks River sank in the ground and rose again some 100 yards below, then flowed southward in a series of rises and sinks-this was a wide, open road with heavy forest growth". It was at this bridge that the Yankees planned to cross and advance up the Plank Road to Tallahassee.

Jacob Gardner, in a letter to his sister dated 13 March 1865 said, "The Yankees received another good drubbing". He went on to relate that "our forces skirmished with them (the Yankees) all morning .... several were killed or wounded, at 11:00 AM., it began in earnest. The fight lasted about 3 1/2 hours ...... mostly an artillery fight. The Second Florida (Confederate)Cavalry came just in time, made a charge, and routed the enemy. The enemy lost, according to their own account, 400 men, every field officer except one killed or wounded. They held some citizens prisoners, but released them. Our force in this battle was about 1000 strong. The enemy numbered 1500."

Confederate losses were three killed, including Captain Henry K. Simmons of Apalachicola whose wife and two-week old son were in Tallahassee. Captain Simmon's body was taken to Tallahassee and buried in the Episcopal Cemetery. Captain Lee Butler was wounded, George Griffin was wounded and lost an arm. There were reportedly thirty-three wounded.

Joshua Frier wrote in his <u>Reminiscences</u> that "the timber in front of us was a sight to me. Many trees of considerable size were cut down at various heights, the limbs and trunks of most of them seemed to have the bark stript from them as by lightening".

There was fierce fighting until about 4:00 in the afternoon when the Yankees gave up the fight and fled back to the East River and their boats. They were repeatedly attacked and harassed by Confederate Cavalry led by Colonel Scott.

And now the Battle was over. In Tallahassee, Susan Bradford Eppes wrote "God has been good to us and the enemy routed".

Sometimes, driving over the Natural Bridge, one who is a little bit fey can <u>almost</u> see the silent forms- gray and blue- slipping through the trees. You must look quickly from the corner of your eye. If you listen closely, you can <u>almost</u> hear the groans of the wounded, the boom of cannon, and the spirited firing of muskets. And far, far away in time, you can <u>almost</u> hear a blood-curdling Rebel yell.

Original Monument at Natural Bridge, Tallahassee, Florida

Current Monument at Natural Bridge

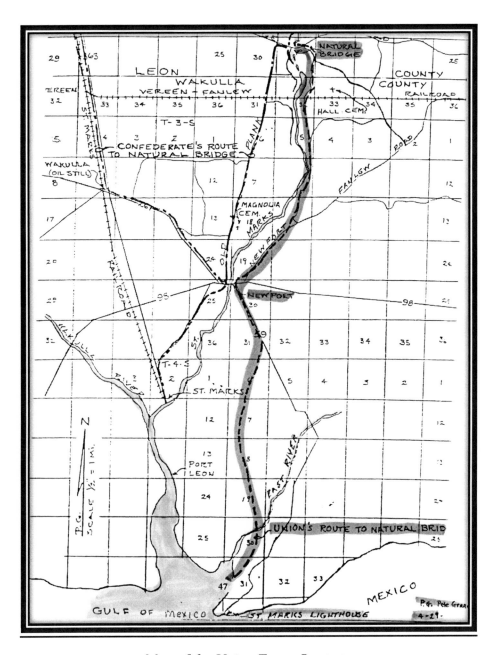

Map of the Union Troop Route to

Natural Bridge

19

Artifacts From The Battle of Natural Bridge

Photos Courtesy (Barnett, 2011)

Union Breast Plate with Bullet Hole found at Burns Place

Cannon Ball Fuses

Military Buttons

20

44 Caliber Pistol- Revolver

Tranter Double Action Revolver (Barnett, 2011)

2 Views of Barrel from above Pistol Showing Damage

Remnants of planks from the old Plank Road that were washed out after a large amount of rain in the 1990s. This occurred prior to the road being surfaced. The road was built in the 1850s as discussed before with the help of Aaron Johnson. Some of the Confederate troops used this road moving to Natural Bridge.

CHAPTER THREE

FAMILY STORIES FROM THE BATTLE OF NATURAL BRIDGE

TG

     This is where our stories begin. After the battle at Newport, the Union sent a few men ahead to scout the area. The remaining army proceeded at a bit slower pace. They were hampered by some wounded and when passing the Stevens homestead decided to drop off some of the wounded. They were left at the Stevens home. The family was told to take good care of the wounded and that they would pick them up later.

     The advance scouts arrived at what is called the Burns Place late the night before the battle. The farm was named for a Matthew Burns who at that time was married to Mary Jane Moore There was a house, a barn and outbuildings in the middle of cleared fields. It was a convenient place for the scouts to overnight and a good spot to use as a staging area for the coming battle. It was almost directly east of the place called Natural Bridge where the scouts hoped to have the Union cross the St Marks River

     At this time James Whaley French lived there. The French and Hall families were friends and neighbors.   Lewis Franklin Hall was staying nearby in March of 1865. He was the great, great grandfather of Pete Gerrell, 5 greats to my grandsons.   He was a confederate soldier and he was home from the war. Family stories vary, He may have been staying at the Burns Place or he may have been at his own home nearby. Marilee Gerrell Butler states, "An interesting thing happened on the way to the Battle of Natural Bridge. Union troops, on their march upriver along the Pinhook Road, took, as prisoner of war, Lewis Franklin Hall, who had been medically discharged from Confederate service earlier. He was down sick with malaria fever, according to family members." (Butler, 1996)

     The Union army was concerned about having an enemy soldier behind them. Even though he was recovering from malaria they were worried he would get word to others about the coming army and hamper their advance. They solved the problem by taking him with them. Lewis Franklin Hall was loaded into the back of a Union wagon on a mattress and taken to the battle. He observed it from the Union side. After the battle when the Union was retreating, they quite politely dropped him back off.

Lewis Franklin Hall

1844-1900

On the other side of the river the Confederates were doing all they could to ready for battle and stop the Union. They already knew where the Union was and what they were trying to do. The number of available men was limited but they began to gather. There were some confederate units including Kilcrease Light Artillery and. Milton's Light Artillery. Both of these units had family members represented in them. George Gerrell was in the Kilcrease Light Artillery and Matthew Burns was in Milton's Light Artillery. The cadets, from what we now know as Florida State, marched down from Tallahassee. And as was common at the time, locals from the area defending their homes also came to engage the Union and protect their homes.

George Edward Gerrell was a member of Kilcrease Light Artillery. Kilcrease Light Artillery was an artillery unit that operated small cannon and was in the area at the time. The Gerrell homes were on the west side of the St. Marks River just a bit north of Natural Bridge. The Gerrell's had an ancestor on both sides of the battle. Remember Lewis Franklin Hall was sick and watching from a Union wagon. George was home from the war visiting with his family. During the war while he had been gone his wife, Margaret, had been taking care of their farm and home. This included George's hunting dogs. The call went out from Tallahassee to all able bodied men about the impending battle. George slept at home that night but got up very early before dawn to go to the battle site at Natural Bridge. Why sleep on the ground when home was so close?

George Edward Gerrell

1833-1872

He was up a couple of hours before dawn and readied his horse. Now, if you have ever been out in the woods or in the river swamp at night or in the early morning, you know that little sounds can seem magnified and carry a great distance. George's hunting hounds got excited. They thought he was getting up to take them hunting and starting barking. He headed to the battle. The hounds became very agitated. The hounds were so excited they managed to escape their pen and they took off through the woods to catch up with George Gerrell on horseback. They caught up with him and followed him all the way to the battle site barking and howling as they went making a terrible racket that carried through the river swamp. It is said that those hounds helped convince the Union to retreat. The Union heard that racket and thought the confederates were getting reinforcements.

As the Union retreated they had to go back the way they came, down the Pinhook road and past the Burns Place. Today this road is called Jim French Rd after one of our ancestors. They were in a hurry as we would expect since they were retreating. On the north side of the road there was a clear sinkhole filled with water. It is said that the Union sank a cannon into that sinkhole. They did not want the Confederates to get access to the cannon and it was slowing down their progress too much to take it with them.

Is there a cannon in that sinkhole?

I, for one, do not know. I do know that since that day the sinkhole has been called Cannon Sink. It is a clear sink that joins the aquifer. My grandsons love to fish for bream in it.

As the Union continued their retreat they retraced their steps. First they went past Cannon Sink, then past the Burns Place and then to return Lewis F. Hall. From there they continued their trek towards the coast. When they went past the Stevens Place again, they picked up the wounded they had dropped off earlier. Three of the wounded had died during the battle. The three were buried on family land. The graves were out in the woods, protected and hidden by our family's ancestors. They wanted to be sure none of the angry locals would desecrate the graves.

Large 100 lb cannon ball.

Found at the Burns Place in 1992

Mystery Cannon Ball-There was no cannon large enough to handle a ball of this size at the battle.

After the war it took a long time for things to settle down. Soldiers were missing and sometimes a family never knew what had happened to a loved one. I'm sure they would have loved a few cell phones in those days. Enoc Hiram Hall was a family member that had fought in The Confederate Army. He had a habit of whistling when he walked. It was some time after the war and the family had not heard from him. Lewis Franklin Hall & Mary Jane were now married. They had talked about him frequently, expressing their desire to hear him whistling once more as he approached. One night very late after they had gone to bed Mary Jane was awakened by a familiar whistle. Very excited she woke her husband, saying "I hear Enoc coming." At first he said, you were just dreaming. She convinced him to listen and after a moment he heard it to. A little while later Enoc came up to the house. He had returned from the war after walking all the way home to Florida. He was only 16 at the end of the war.

There is another family civil war story that has always caught my interest. It can leave you wondering about the determination and fortitude of the people of the time. Daniel B. Coleman was a young commissioned officer in the Confederate Army. He was 30 years old and a Captain in the Confederacy, something for his family to be proud of at the time. He was the brother of John Coleman. John was married to Mary Hall and that is how he came to be family. Mary was the youngest daughter of Elizabeth Byrd Hall.

He was stationed in Pensacola Florida. In this day and time we think of that as nearby, just 3½ hours or so to get there. In 1862, he may as well have been in Washington D.C. Daniel became ill of an infectious disease. Here, family stories vary; perhaps he had malaria, yellow fever, or diphtheria. Now, we will never know. He died in 1862 in Pensacola from his illness. A senseless death, not related to the war at all. And yet, if not for the war, would he have fallen ill?

They wanted to bury him near his family. The soldiers and army needed a way to transport him back to Tallahassee. Remember Florida and our heat, slow transportation and no air conditioning. How to do this without infecting anyone else or having the body decay and smell too much during transportation?

The answer was to place him in the back of a wooden wagon. They covered his body in coal. The thought was that this would keep down the smell and decay as well as preventing the spread of any infection. They did get him back to Tallahassee. Then the family had to decide what to do to bury him without risking infection. They decided to bury the whole wagon. The wheels were removed and he was buried in the wagon of coal in the Hall Place Cemetery. This cemetery is one of the oldest in Wakulla County and is still located on family land. His grave is well marked with a marker and the stump of a long dead tree. There is now a smaller tree growing out of the original stump.

Recently (the Sons of The Confederacy Camp Cresset #1614) Finley's Brigade dedicated some new headstones to the four veterans of the Civil War know to be buried in the Hall Place Cemetery. Research obtained from them shows Daniel Boone Coleman was born in Georgia in or around 1830. In 1853 he married Christianna Ella Yonge in Jackson County Florida. They lived in Marianna Florida at the time the war started where Daniel was a salesman. Their children were Hannie, Addie, & Jennie.

Daniel enlisted in the Confederate Army in March of 1862 at Bluff Springs near Pensacola. He was a member of the First Florida Infantry, Company I. Records show he died June 25, 1862 with an infectious disease of the throat. The family then moved to Alabama.

Daniel had a brother as previously mentioned, John Coleman. John was born in Georgia in 1837. There may have been two additional brothers, William and Patrick Henry. John lived in St. Marks Florida and was a farmer in 1860. He married Mary Hall, the youngest daughter of Enoch and Elizabeth Hall. He was 6'1" with dark hair and blue eyes.

John enlisted at Camp Leon near Tallahassee, Florida. He was a member of the Fifth Florida Infantry Company I, also known as the Wakulla Tigers. He was a Private. Private Coleman did some traveling in the war. He was at the Battle of Cedar Mountain and the Battle of Manassas. In October of 1862 he was hospitalized and sent home to Tallahassee. He did return to his unit but the timing of this is unclear. He was also involved in the Siege of Petersburg and some battles near Richmond Virginia. We believe he was killed in action in Virginia in 1864 or 1865.

Another soldier buried at the Hall place Cemetery is Lafayette G. Moore. His date of birth was around 1838. He lived near Natural Bridge. It is thought he was related to Mary Jane Moore, the widow of Matthew Burns and second wife of Lewis F. Hall. He joined the army on July 8, 1861 in Tallahassee, Florida. He was part of Company D of the Second Florida Infantry. Captain Theodore Brevard was his commander. The unit left Tallahassee and went to Jacksonville were they were officially mustered into the Confederate Army. He went from there to Richmond Virginia arriving July 21, 1861. He became ill quickly and was hospitalized. He was an early war casualty. He died in the Confederate Hospital on September 7, 1861.

The last of our four Civil War soldiers is Matthew Burns. He was born in 1842 in Alabama. On May 9, 1858 he married Mary Jane Moore in Leon County, Florida. They had two children, John born in 1859 and Josephine born in 1860.They lived on what is still family land and still called the Burns Place.

Matthew Burns enlisted in Apalachicola, Florida on March 10, 1862 in Milton's Light Artillery. He was a Private. His unit was involved in engagements that defended the St. Johns River in and around Jacksonville, Florida. He was at the Battle of Olustee in February, 1864.

His unit was also here to defend his home at the Battle of Natural Bridge. After Natural Bridge he and his unit went to Savannah and from there to the Carolinas. In April 1865, he was one of the soldiers surrendered with the Army of Tennessee at Greensboro, North Carolina. His military records show him present for every roll call. Matthew died shortly after the war in 1865 at the age of 23. His wife, Mary Jane, later married Lewis Franklin Hall, another veteran of the war.

Pete Gerrell 1992

After digging up a cannon ball buried 3 feet deep

At the Burns Homestead

The family still owns the staging area, called The Burns Place, and some of the land between there and Natural Bridge where the battle took place. We know the stories and we know the route the union took. Over the years an occasional artifact was found. In the 1990s my husband and I spent some time exploring and excavating parts of the Burns Place. We found many holes with civil war artifacts buried in them. We will never know how they got buried in holes. Perhaps the family cleaned up after the battle and buried them to get them out of the way. It would have been hard to farm or plow a field with cannon balls and gun barrels in it. The artifacts are owned by PG Artifacts LLC. The majority of the artifacts have been documented by a Master's student at

Florida State University (Barnett, 2011). She has graciously granted permission for me to include the listing of the artifacts that she compiled from her thesis work as well as some photos The artifact listing will be placed as Appendix A at the end of this text. Several photos of the artifacts can be seen in Appendix B.

There was a period after the civil war known as the Reconstruction Era. In times past the family has held this story close and been careful with the telling. Now however, its time is long past. No one can be hurt by it and it should be written before it is lost. The Gerrell siblings have allowed me to write about it here.

There was a Clerk of Courts in Wakulla County by the name of John Hogue. The local government was corrupt and he was in the thick of it. Taxes were heavy and sometimes double assessed. It was thought that he kept two sets of books or just never recorded certain things. The citizens were upset and hurting financially. The economy was already bad enough during that period. Many wanted something done. A group of five prominent men in the county banded together to deal with the situation.

The family story alleges that James Whaley French was one of the five men. Each of the men had a part to play in the drama. It was decided they should kill John Hogue. Everyone had a different role to fill and no one knew who was doing what and when. One man provided the gun, one the ammunition, one loaded the gun, one provided the horse, and one was to pull the trigger. They drew straws to determine who would do what.

They came very close to being discovered. The death occurred later than it was supposed to. One of the men involved in an earlier part of the plan was on the road out of Crawfordville. He passed a man going the opposite direction and asked him if he had heard that John Hogue and been killed. When the man got to town, old John Hogue was still alive, however he was killed later that day.

H. Clay Crawford wrote an account of this event in his memoirs that is somewhat confusing. He also states the Ku Klux Klan was involved. Mr. Crawford was born in 1856. This makes him age 9 when the war ended and a young teen during reconstruction. Chances are his telling was also not 100% accurate. Our family version is a bit different and does not include anything like that. The truth is, we may never know exactly how it happened; only that it did. Crawford's account also indicates the man on the road may have been Lawrence Council and they were talking about a man by the name of Henderson who also died. Our story again, differs a bit here.

We do know that shortly after the incident, James Whaley French moved across the county line and changed his name for a while. It is said in the family that he did that to avoid trouble and scandal after the murder. He is listed in the 1870 census as James W. Cato. The names and ages of his wife and family remained the same except for the last name which was also changed to Cato. In later years he and the family returned to the original name of French.

As I'm sure you realize by now this families history revolves around Natural Bridge, The St. Marks River and Wakulla & Leon Counties in North Florida. In 1922 James and Mary French decided to give two acres of land at Natural Bridge to The Daughters of the Confederacy to commemorate the Civil War Battlefield and preserve it for future generations. A copy of the deeds wording follows. Note that distances are measured in chains. A portion of a survey chain was found at the Hall family home site. Just perhaps it was part of the survey chain used to measure the family lands or the Natural Bridge land deeded to The Daughters of the Confederacy

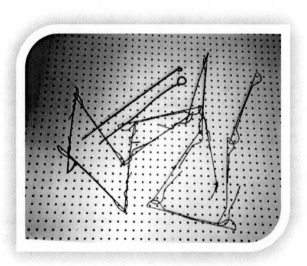

Portion of Survey Chain and Two Pins Found at Hall Place Home Site.

Kilcrease Light Artillery Re-Enactors c. 1995

Pete Gerrell excavating an artifact hole on family land

DEED
BATTLE FIELD OF NATURAL BRIDGE, LEON COUNTY, FLORIDA

This indenture made this the 4th day of March, A.D. 1922, between James R. French and Mary A. French, his wife, of the County of Wakulla, in the State of Florida, parties of the first part, and Sallie A. Lewis, Mrs. J. Stuart Lewis, President of Anna Jackson Chapter, United Daughters of the Confederacy, and her successors in office of the County of Leon, in the State of Florida, party of the second part, Witnesseth.

That the said parties of the first part, for and in consideration of the sum of One Dollar ($1.00) to each of them in hand paid by the said party of the second part, the receipt whereof is hereby acknowledged, and to aid the purposes designed and intended to be accomplished by the Act of the Legislature of Florida, hereinafter mentioned, have granted, bargained and sold unto the said party of the second part, her successors, in office and assigns, in trust for the purpose of establishing and maintaining a suitable park and erecting a monument and memorial at the scene of the Battle of Natural Bridge, in Leon County, Florida, as contemplated by an Act of the Legislature of Florida of 1921 known as Chapter 8433 Laws of Florida, and entitled "An Act to make an appropriation to assist in the erection of a monument-and establishing a park on the Battle Field, of Natural Bridge, in Leon County, Florida, "The following described land situate, lying and being in the County of Leon and in the State of Florida, to wit:

Commence at the Southeast corner of the Northeast Quarter of the North west Quarter of Section Twenty-Nine (29) in Township Two (2) South of Range two (2) East, thence run North three and sixteen one-hundreths, 3.16 chains, thence East four and fifty one-hundreths, 4.50 chains, to the East Bank of the Saint Marks River. Commence again at the Southeast corner of the Northeast Quarter of the Northwest Quarter of Section Twenty-Nine (29) in Township Two (2) South Range Two (2) East, thence run South three and sixteen one-hundreths, 3.16 chains, thence East five (5) chains to the East Bank of the Saint Marks River, thence Northerly along the East Bank of said Saint Marks River to a point three and sixteen one-hundreths 3.16 chains North and four and fifty one-hundreths 4.50 chains East of the Southeast corner of the

Northeast Quarter of the Northwest Quarter of said Section Twenty-Nine (29) in Township Two (2) South of Range Two (2) East, containing two acres, more or less.

TO HAVE AND TO HOLD the said granted premises unto the said party of the second part and her successors, in office and assigns, for the uses and purposes and upon the trusts declared in and by the Act of the Legislature of the State of Florida aforesaid.

And the said parties of the first part do hereby fully warrant the title to said land, as against themselves and their heirs, and all persons claiming by or through or under them and each of them, and will defend the same against the lawful claims of all persons, claiming by, through or under them and each of them.

In witness thereof, the said parties of the first part have hereunto set their hands and seals this the day and year first above written.

J. R. French_____

     (SEAL)

Mary A. French_____

    ____(SEAL)

Signed, sealed and delivered in our presence.

F. C. Williamson_____

L. L. Lewis_____

State of Florida,
County of Leon,

I hereby certify that on this the 4th day of March A.D. 1922, before me, an officer authorized to take acknowledgements of deeds according to the laws of the State of Florida, duly qualified and acting personally appeared James R. French, and Mary A. French, his wife, to me well known to be the persons described in and who executed the foregoing instrument of writing and severally acknowledged that they executed the same as and for their own free act and deed and for the uses and purposes therein expressed, and the said Mary A. French, upon a private examination, separately and apart from her husband, then and there acknowledged before me that she executed the said instrument of writing freely and voluntarily, and without compulsion, constraint, apprehension or fear of or from her husband, for the purpose of relinquishing, renouncing, releasing and conveying all her right, title and interest, whether of dower or right of dower, separate estate and homestead rights, or of any nature whatsoever, in and to the "lands and tenements therein described.

IN WITNESS WHEREOF, I have hereunto set my hand and seal this the 4th day of March A.D. 1922.

F. C.
Williamson,

(SEAL)Notary Public in and for the State of Florida at large, My Commission expires on the 23rd of January A.D. 1926.

State of Florida, County of Leon,

BE IT REMEMBERED, that on this 10th day of March A.D. 1923 the foregoing instrument of writing was presented for record to the subscriber, Clerk of the Circuit Court in and for the County aforesaid, and the same being properly authenticated, I have duly recorded the same.

IN WITNESS WHEREOF, I have hereunto set my hand and the seal of said Court, the day and year last above written.

DAVE LANG

_____Clerk

CHAPTER FOUR

JIM FRENCH TG

James Whaley French had been married to Emmaree Duggar. They had two children, William and James W. James or Jim as he was known stayed in this area.

Jim French was a well respected man during his life. He was a farmer, a woodsman, fisherman, hunter, a surveyor, and livestock inspector to name a few of his professions through the years, In short he was a North Florida native who could live off the land and did what he needed to do at the time to survive. As most people during his time, he was flexible. His preference however, was to stay at home on his land and in his woods. Whenever possible he could be found working his own land to provide.

Jim French was on his own at an early age. He attended the Florida Normal School in Defuniak Springs. He earned a Teachers Certificate while there. In 1899 Jim French came to teach at the County Line School on the line between Leon & Wakulla counties. He lived at this time with the Hall Family. Lewis Franklin and Mary Jane took him as a boarder. While there he met his future wife.

Jim French married Mary Ann Mariah (Mollie) Hall on July 7, 1901. The Frenches settled on the St. Marks River near Mollie's childhood home. Mollie wore a beautiful black brocade skirt on the day of her wedding. The wedding license was issued by Wakulla County Judge McLeod. They were married on July 7, 1901.

Mollies father, Lewis died shortly after the marriage and she inherited some land and livestock. Throughout their lives Jim & Mollie continued to invest in nearby lands and additional livestock. They had five lovely daughters. Elsie, Frank, Ina, Jessie, and Nina.

<u>*Black Brocade Wedding Skirt of Mollie Hall French*</u>

"The bodice of the elegant ensemble has been lost. It was of the same black brocade fabric, with long pointed sleeves and a stand up collar. Bodice and skirt were lined with brown sateen. Black was a fashionable color for wedding apparel at the turn of the century. The marriage was performed by Minister Thomas Isler, relative of the bride at the home of the bride."

Quote from Marilee Gerrell Butler

Wedding License Jim & Mollie French

1ˢᵗ Home Of Jim & Mollie French at St. Marks River
Photo taken of painting by Frank F. Blackburn 1991

Jim and Mollie originally built a home near the St. Marks River just a short distance from Mollie's family home. It was a modest four room house. (Photo to follow) They began to have their family. Four of the family's daughters were born in that home

Mollie taught school at the Pinhook School and later at Oil Still Station where relative Ahijah had once owned and run a turpentine still. She became known for helping the sick in 1905 during a diphtheria epidemic. She would go to people's homes and help them in whatever little ways she could. According to her grandchildren, she continued this practice throughout her life.

The family dreamed of a bigger home. In 1915 plans for this home and the building of it began. It was two stories with a full length upper and lower front porch. The final daughter Nina was born in this home in 1917.

The family was growing and secure. For the era 1930-1940s during the depression, they were financially sound although not rich. Later as you read thorough some of the stories Pete wrote about growing up here, you will hear him talk about three houses and Granddaddy's cottage and the things that happened there. So now I'd like to tell you about the third house and how that came to be.

First a quick reminder; the Gerrell branch of the family lived on farmland about 3 miles from Woodville off of Natural Bridge Rd. The Frenches' were located on the east side of the river, another 3 ½ miles or so further from Woodville. Jim French, known as Granddaddy to Pete Marilee, Dale & Lawson also had a small cottage or cabin closer to the river he used.

The house in Woodville came into existence when Nina was about six or seven years old. Nina French was going to school at the Woodville School on the corner of Woodville Highway and Natural Bridge. The bus would pick her up where the family's mailbox was on Natural Bridge 6-7 miles from Woodville. It took her to school and each day at the end of the day she would be dropped back off there. Nina's daddy, Jim French would pick her up there and take her on to the house, a mile or so down the river. One afternoon when he went to get her, Nina was nowhere to be found and the bus was not running late.

Home Of Jim & Mollie French built 1915.

Jim started a hunt for his daughter. The bus driver at the time was Pop Niblett. Jim went to his Pop Nibletts' home. At that time the bus driver took the bus to his house at the end of the day. Nina was found on the bus. She had fallen asleep and no one knew she was still on the bus.

Jim French decided then and there that such a thing would not happen again. He shortly thereafter found and bought a house in Woodville. It was located near Woodville Highway on property that now belongs to the First Baptist Church. This was at most a block from the school and Nina could now walk back and forth without worrying about buses. Mollie and the children starting living in town, Woodville, during the week.

NAMING A CYPRESS POND   <u>TG</u>

Jessie French was born May 1, 1910. She was the fourth of the five children. Once she was old enough, it was Jessie's job to take her Daddy his lunch and fresh water when he was out working in the fields or the woods. This usually required a little hike to wherever he was working, sometimes a distance of a mile or more. The sheep pasture and some of the fields were east of the house. To get to them Jessie had to pass by a cypress pond. This cypress pond covers 2-4 acres. There are times when it has just has a few inches of water and at other times it is several feet deep. It was and is full of lovely old cypress trees and surrounded by old live oak trees. All the trees were draped with gray Spanish moss. On the sunniest of days, it can still be shady and dark with shadows cast from above.

Imagine how Jessie felt at age 6 or 7 when she had to go past that pond to take Dad his lunch. One time some of the family cows came running out of the pond and scared her. She climbed a pine tree still hanging onto that water bucket. Some tree bark from the climb fell into the water. Later she was asked how the bark got into the water. She explained and said, "I was afraid a boogar was going to come out and get me." After that she was sometimes afraid of the shadows and shapes. She took to running past this area as fast as she could. The pond was dubbed The Booger Pond and is called that to this day.

Jessie started school at the Pinhook Schoolhouse about 1 ½ miles east of her home. She went there from 1916-1920. For her second year of school, she and her older sisters went to school in Newport. Newport was a fair distance, too far to walk every day through the woods. The girls boarded with the Karl family during the week. They would come home on the weekends.

GRANDDADDY'S COTTAGE   <u>PG</u>

Granddaddy kind of liked to stay alone, kind of like me, a loner; he kind of liked to be by himself. He would stay over in the old cottage on the river. He wouldn't stay in the big house, which is not a hundred yards from the cottage. He stayed in the cottage that had nothing but one room and two beds in it. Anyway, I'd come back from down at the lighthouse or wherever I had been cow hunting that day and would ride into Granddaddy's house. He always had a little something to eat. We'd eat some supper and he'd ask me if mamma knew where I was. "No, I don't reckon she does, Granddaddy, but she don't worry about me anyway. She knows I'm all right." So I'd just stay there and spend the night with Granddaddy.

Granddaddy had always wanted a boy. In fact, he had five girls and the first one he named Elsie. The second one he named Ina. Then another girl came along and he named it after his daddy-in-law, Frank. And that was her name. It wasn't Frances, it was Frank. Anyway, my mother came along and he named her Jessie. I don't know whether that was after Jesse James or who it was after, but he still wanted him a boy. Then, my youngest aunt came along in about 1916 and he named her Nina, but he called her Buck. So, he never had his boy.

There was only one grandson that was older than me, David, and he lived in Sylvania, Georgia, so he wasn't that close to Granddaddy. (David Blackburn, son of Frank French Blackburn) He would come down and spend a lot of time with him during the summer, but I spent just about all my time with Granddaddy on the river. We were always together. He gave me his favorite horse, Blue Pete, when he quit riding. He would take his naps in the afternoon. He'd take an old straight chair, lay it on the porch, turn it upside down with the back of the chair sloping down, and then he would lay down on that and sleep on that chair. He would take his afternoon siesta on that chair.

We went many times through the woods, with him showing me the different things. He had had about three hundred head of sheep at one time and there were still a few of them in the woods. The rustlers finally got all of them except for two or three that were left there. I remember the old sheep that were left there. They would come back to the pasture in the wintertime. They'd come home, and I remember two or three of them still being there and finally there was only one left. Granddaddy would go through, looking at his sheep and he would ride the woods, looking at his cows. He had an old '37 Ford pick-up truck by then. He rode it like he rode a horse. You never knew where the roads were, he just took off through the woods in it. The woods were burned over and fairly open then because of the Turpentine operations that were going on in them. Also, the freshening up of the ranges for keeping the grass green for the cows and the burning of the woods kept it fairly open. So, he would just take off across the woods and be riding along, saying "Rough road, isn't it boys?" We were not even on a road riding through the woods.

Anyway, Granddaddy was quite a character and he stayed in the woods and took care of his animals. He'd never go to eat supper himself or eat a meal himself without making sure that his animals were fed first. His animals had to be fed.

Jim French on his porch

The wild hogs, of course we didn't worry about whether they were feeding or not because we would put the dogs after them and catch them and then tie them down. In the hunting of deer, bear, squirrels, anything like that, any of the game animals, we would go usually on south moon over or south moon under, which was the major feed time. On the part of the cows, we would hunt cows during the major feed time, too and find them standing up. You did see them standing up feeding during that time.

The moon was used to judge when we did things. We also used the Almanac and went by the different signs to tell when to mark and brand the calves or mark the hogs and things of that type. Anything that was related to any wounds that might cause an animal to bleed, such as marking the ears, you'd always want the signs to be in the legs. We'd go by the Almanac on that and where the signs were so we wouldn't injure the animals too severely. Believe it or not, it was a true thing. When the signs were in the lower part of the body or down into the legs, the animals would not bleed near as much from being marked. We had to mark the animals because it was the only way we would tell whose animals were whose. So we would take and mark them when they were calves. I'll get more into that later.

We also didn't have any way to tell the time except by the sun and possibly by the moon at night if we knew what phase it was in. We would be able to tell the time by the sun and that was the only way we had of telling how long it would be before the sun set or noon or whenever. We didn't carry watches. In the case of Granddaddy's old cottage, he didn't even have a clock in it. He did have one up at the house, but he didn't have one down at the cottage where we stayed most of the time. He taught me how to tell time by the sun and using the hand to judge how many hours it would be before noon or sunset, how late it was in the morning by telling how high the sun was above the morning horizon.

Talking about Granddaddy staying at the cottage, there were several things there at the cottage that were sort of amazing to watch the way Granddaddy took care of them. One was rattlesnake rattlers. When he'd kill a rattlesnake, he would hang the rattlers up from the front porch rafters. Anytime one of the children started to play with those rattlers, he'd tell them not to play with them because they would cause you to go blind if you got the dust of the rattlesnake rattlers in your eyes. I don't know if there is any truth to it or not, but I'm sure there wasn't because I'd probably have been blind at the age of seven or eight if there had been any truth to it. But it kept us away from playing with his rattlesnake rattlers, anyway. Why he kept them there I don't really know except maybe just to give us something to amuse us. He was real good at that.

Rattlesnake Rattlers Collected Over The Years

He also took great care of his spiders and his lizards. The spiders had webs everywhere in the old cabin and they were protected and you didn't do anything to bother them. If they abandoned their web, we would take a long pole and wind the web up on the end of the pole and take it down, but as long as it was an active spider web, you wouldn't bother it. That was the way the spiders caught the bugs and we didn't want to do anything to increase the population of bugs, so we increased the population of the spiders. The lizard was about the same way, only he didn't have a web. He just sat around in places and stuck his tongue out and caught the bugs. The toad frog lived under the house usually and we didn't bother him either. He was a bug catcher and we were told to protect him as well as the lizards and spiders.

Another thing about the spiders, their web was used as a means of stopping bleeding. If you had a cut on you and the blood wouldn't clot, you'd take a spider web and put it on. That would stop the bleeding. I remember Granddaddy getting cut across the calf of his leg by a hog that caught him. He got cut real bad across the calf of his leg and he took some spider webs and put them in it to stop the bleeding as well as putting kerosene on it. After he got it cleaned out and the bleeding stopped, he put benzoin, which was his favorite type of medicine, on it and wrapped it up in a clean rag.

THE BOAR HOG THAT MARKED GRANDDADDY   <u>PG</u>

I often spent time with my granddaddy at his old "hunting camp," a cottage on the St. Marks River. He had two big houses but preferred to stay on the front porch of the cottage where he could watch the river flow by. I would ride my horse over there to the cottage about four miles from my other granddaddy's house where we lived. The trip required crossing the river with a horse. After granddaddy turned the basin cows into their calves, and fed and watered our horses, we would just sit on the porch and visit. No one lived nearer than my other granddaddy so we were totally alone. Might best tell you, I had a grandmamma too but she lived in the big house in town. At about sundown, granddaddy would say, "boy, does your Mammy know where you are?' I would say yes sir, when I don't get home by dark she will know I'm with you.

We were sitting on the porch watching the river flow by one evening when we heard old Jake, granddaddies hog dog barking. He was about a quarter mile down the river swamp so we headed out to see what he had bayed. When we got to Jake we could see that he had a big boar hog backed up in a Palmetto patch on the edge of the swamp. Being the fall of the year it was time to start catching hogs and shutting them up to fatten for killing during winter. The boars made good sausage meat if they were castrated, then left penned up to fatten for a couple of months. Granddaddy, being over 70 years old, didn't have any business trying to catch a 150 pound wild boar hog, but he knew no fear. Instead of him catching the hog, the hog caught him and opened a large gash across the calf of his right leg. That quarter-mile back to the cottage with granddaddy was one of the longest trips I ever made and I'm sure it was even longer for him.

He was still bleeding when we finally made it to the cottage. He instructed me to get a stick and roll up some spider webs on it. There were plenty of spider webs in the rafters of the cottage. After getting a bundle of webs on the end of the stick, we put it into the open cut. This caused the blood to clot and stopped the bleeding. He told me to get one of the kerosene lamps from inside the cottage and he opened the lamp and poured the kerosene on the cut. According to him, this would disinfect it. After the kerosene sat a few minutes, he cleaned it off, put benzoin on it and wrapped it up with a clean rag. The cut was about four inches long and 1 1/2 inches deep. It must have bled a quart. By the time he got his wound dressed, if you could call that rag a dressing, it was after dark. We decided to stay at the cottage overnight and make the dirt road eight mile trip to grandma's the next morning. Several times during the night I heard granddaddy groan and I knew he must be in severe pain. He had taken several big shots of whiskey before going to bed. I'm sure that helped to get him through the night.

The next morning we started up the old '37 Ford pickup, and went to see grandmamma. She redressed the wound and we stayed at her house until the local doctor came that evening. He lived just across the railroad from Grandmamma's. The doctor sewed granddaddies hog mark up but he carried the scar for the rest of his life. A few days later Daddy, old Jake, and I caught that boar, made a gentleman of him, and removed his tusks with a crowbar, hammer and chisel. We then left him in the pen to fatten.

Woodville Home of Mollie Hall French

CHAPTER FIVE

GROWING UP IN WAKULLA AND LEON COUNTIES <u>TG</u>

NOVEMBER 26, 1932

During the fall of the year in 1932, people in Wakulla and Leon counties were spending time getting ready for winter. These were hard years in the area. Folks were suffering with the rest of the country during the depression. People worked the land and did what they had to do to provide for themselves. Sweeteners such as sugar were expensive and luxuries most folks did not spend money on or couldn't get. During the summer the cane crop that year grew well. It was harvested and was ready now to be cooked into syrup. Cane syrup could be put up and used all year as a sweetener when cooking. It was the source of one of the children's favorite treats; **Holey Boleys.** Take a biscuit, poke a hole in it with your finger, fill it with cane syrup and you have a happy sticky child. Cane syrup could also be a valuable money crop during the era. In a time when sugar and other sweeteners were hard to come by it could be sold as a cash crop. The moon shiners paid well for it so they could make the whiskey that provided for their livelihood.

On the morning of Nov 26, 1932, Jessie French Gerrell went to her parent's home on the east side of the St. Marks River to help with the syrup cooking. She was nine months pregnant with her second child. She spent the day helping with the cooking of the cane syrup and putting it up for the year. The work was hot and heavy but it needed to be done. Towards the end of the day the weather was changing and a storm moved in. At day's end Jessie went home to the west side of the river where she and her husband Walter were living with his parents. The Gerrell home had recently burned down and the family was alternating living part time in the barn and living with nearby relatives while a new home was built.

Upon her return home she went into the barn and went into labor. She gave birth to her second child that stormy night. When the child was born Jessie discussed his name with her husband Walter. She wanted to name him for each of his grandfathers. He was the first male child born to the couple. He had one older sister at the time, Marilee Gerrell. Jessie chose Allen Roston Gerrell; Allen for his paternal grandfather and Roston for his maternal grandfather. Walter told Jessie that the name was fine with him. She could call him whatever she wanted, he however, was going to call the child "Pete." He was legally named Allen Roston Gerrell but from that day on he was always called PETE. She once told me she knew when he was born on a stormy night that he would have a stormy life. He was known for being a go getter. He was frequently involved in change or controversy. People loved him or disliked him intensely.

Gerrell Home built in1933

Used by the family until 1970s

MAKING CANE SYRUP   <u>PG</u>

Almost all of the farms and homesteads in our area had patches of cane and depended on the cane for their source of sweeteners for most things. They also used some to sell. We happened to have a cane patch too. An old mule pulled a mill that ground the cane. We would cook the syrup in a kettle. The cane patch was put into the new ground area, which was where we had penned the cows up last spring. Then we'd plant the cane in it. It would grow there for several years. You could just leave what we would call the stubbles and burn it off in the spring. The cane would come right back up and grow again. We really raised some big patches of cane.

One of the big things at the cane grinding after we stripped and chapped the cane and hauled it into the mill on the old wagon was the fun that we had socializing and playing on the pummie pile. The pummie pile was the crushed stalks of cane after they had gone through the mill. The mule was hitched to the mill by way of a small pine tree that went across the top of the mill and went down. The mule pulled the mill by that. All he did was walk around and around all day.

One of the big things was to watch this mule until you got drunk watching him go around and around. I know he must have been worse off than we were by having to walk like that all day long.

After the cane was ground through the mill, the juice went through a screen and was filtered. Then it went into a barrel. From there, it was moved to the kettle. The first charge of the day to go into the kettle (putting it in was called "charging the kettle") was usually done a few minutes after daylight. The kettle held 60 or 80 gallons, according to what size it was. We had an 80 gallon kettle. Fire was built under the kettle. The kettle was put into a brick furnace like area. Someone had to tend the fire most all day to keep the fire going. We would cook off as many as three charges a day on a good day. We had to keep the fire going and the juice boiling, which was the process of boiling the water out of the juice.

There was someone that had to stay with the skimmer during the cooking and keep the impurities skimmed off the top. This was kept and put in a barrel, which was later fed to the hogs. It took a person knowing what to do and how to do it. The experienced person doing the cooking had gained his knowledge of what to do and when to do it, how much fire to have under the kettle, when to build it up and when to draw it out by simple experience and watching the older folks do it. He came up with it and that was just part of it.

After it was made, the syrup was put into bottles or cans or both. We used gallon sized cans to put the syrup in that was to be sold. We sold mostly to the moon shiners who used it to make their whiskey with it. The syrup that we were going to use to eat or sell to others, we would put into bottles. They were usually reprocessed drink bottles, such as whiskey bottles or soda water bottles or whatever bottles we could get. We hardly ever used anything with a big top. It was always a smaller topped bottle for some reason or other. I never asked or knew why. We usually made syrup for about a week, which should make up several hundred gallons, maybe three hundred gallons of syrup to last us through the year.

I had an Uncle Rainey. Mr. Johnny and Uncle Rainey were noted for the whiskey stills. Right after the no fence law came in effect it rained for several months. I went downstream from Uncle Rainey's whiskey still after the creeks went back into their banks. The sides of the creeks were lined with gallon syrup buckets and moonshine jugs. That was one of our main outlets of sale for syrup, especially during the war. You could let the syrup sit in the syrup house for six or eight months and it would actually crystallize and the sugar would be in the bottom of the buckets. They would actually have sugar to make the moonshine out of.

There was one by product from the syrup making that always was a comedy to me. When you fed it to the hogs, they would get drunk. It was cane buck that was the fermented skimmings off the syrup as it cooked in the kettle. They'd put the skimmings in a barrel and let it ferment, then draw off the bottom of it and we'd take it and pour it into the hog trough and let the hogs drink it. We'd have a pen full of hogs that were almost fat enough for killing and butchering. The old hogs would get drunk and fall all over each other and squeal and carry on. It reminded me of some of the things you see in this day and time in the bars with people - the way the hogs would get drunk and squeal and fall on each other and wallow around in the mud.

Anyway, every once in a while we would decide we wanted to take a drink of this cane buck too. One time I was going to the cattle camp down on the Wacissa River on the western sloughs. I was getting ready to go in the morning. We had loaded the wagon and got it ready to go to the western sloughs and we had some cane buck in the barrel that had worked off real good. I got me a big glass of it, along with another one of the boys that was going to the camp with us. We got us a glass of that and drank it and I stayed awake most of the night. The next morning I had to get the mules hooked to the wagon. It was a two mule wagon. We got the mules hooked to the wagon and we started to the woods. I was kind of glad I was in the woods because I had to stop several times because of what that cane buck had done to my stomach. I got down to about eight miles from home and the mules run over a stump with the wagon and broke the axle and it was almost a blessing that we broke it.

The other boy took the two mules and went back the eight miles and got another wagon and brought it back. You can picture how long I sat there waiting for him. I was about a miserable soul that day. That broke me up from drinking cane buck. I decided I never wanted to drink anymore of that.

LIVING AT THE WOODVILLE HOUSE <u>PG</u>

In my early years, during the time I was growing up, we didn't have the convenience of electricity, telephones or electric or gas stoves. We had to use kerosene lamps for our light and wood stoves for cooking on. We did have two fireplaces in the house. I say in the house - we had two houses, or three houses. One was Grandma French's house in town, Woodville. Then there was Grandma and Granddaddy Gerrell's house that was about 31/2 miles into the piney woods country down Natural Bridge. Then there was Granddaddy French's house east of the river, another six miles into the piney woods country.

We lived at Grandma French's house up until the war came along in 1941. Some of the exciting things that came along during the time we were at Grandma French's house in town were such things as Mr. Ashburn's Rolling Store. We always got to buy candy from him. From the looks of it he must have had some of everything in the back of his old truck. Thinking of it now, it was probably the nearest thing in those days to what we would now call a hippie van. Anyway, if we needed something he didn't have, he would take an order and bring it on the next trip through. I don't remember how often he came by, only it wasn't often enough for a small boy.

Another great convenience we had was the fish man. He would come through about once a week during the mullet running season. We didn't have refrigerators to keep food fresh, so Mamma would always buy fish on the day the fish man came and fry them on the stove.

I said we didn't have refrigerators, so I'd better tell you what we did have to keep the food cold. We had an ice box that sat on the back porch. It hardly held enough ice to last between trips of the ice man. The ice man came through twice a week in his truck making deliveries. He carried big blocks of ice with white streaks running through. Where the white streaks were is where he would hit it with his pick or tongs and break the blocks into 25 or 50 pound blocks. We usually got 50 pounds. This was all the old ice box would hold.

Sometimes Mamma would get 25 pounds extra and we would make some ice cream with the old hand cranked ice cream freezer. Boy that stuff was plumb good. There'd always have to be a fight over who was going to lick the churn after the ice cream was done.

54

When the ice man picked the ice to break it, some pieces just the right size for eating would break off. That's why you would see all the children in the neighborhood following the iceman around. Some people said that the children followed the iceman around cause they thought he was their daddy. That wasn't the reason why I was following him around - because he was the wrong color to be mine.

I mentioned the old wood stove. It was our only source of hot water. It had a reservoir mounted on the side of the stove, usually on the left side, but, it could be swapped to the right. It held about ten gallons. The water had to be carried in and put into it by the buckets full from outside at the old pitcher pump. Also, there was a kettle that held about a gallon of water that sat on the big stove all the time. My favorite place to do my school homework was behind the wood stove, sitting on the floor. That was the warmest place in the house in the wintertime. Also, the lamp sat on top of the stove warmer, so that was the place with a little light too.

Kerosene Lamps & Candles Were Light Sources

I can't remember many times that the old wood stove got cool. It almost always had some hot coals in the firebox. That's another job that was always waiting for me to do too. I had to bring in the wood for the old wood stove and fill up the wood box. About the time I got the wood box full, I was told to take out the ashes. So, I had to empty out the ashes from the old stove and carry them outside. They were usually put around the pecan trees to help fertilize them.

One of the most fun times I had playing was playing in the rain. We had a gutter that came off the house and the rain fell under the gutter and made a big hole in the ground. I was standing there making mud pies and what we called "frog houses" out of the mud that was built up around that place where the gutter had made the hole in the ground. I stuck my foot into one of my frog houses and was wiggling it around and my sister had one of her usual weapons that she used. It was a shovel. She saw my foot wiggling around in the frog house and hit it with the shovel. It hit my big toe and if there had been a doctor around to take stitches, he could have sewed all day on the cut that she put in my toe.

The place we took our bath was down close to the pond. We had a pump down there with an old sugar kettle under it. Whether it was winter or summer, we would pump that sugar kettle full of cold water and get in it to take a bath. That was the extent of our washing. Many times when we might have been sent down there by Mamma to wash, we didn't get but part of the way, we played around a little bit and then went back to the house. But she did an under arm and behind the ear inspection on us and checked us out and then would send us back, so that didn't work.

White Primitive Baptist Church

Circa 1940s

CHURCH <u>PG</u>

My family belonged to the local Primitive Baptist Church and we usually went to church on Sunday morning. I didn't care a whole lot about going to church in those days because the preachers were all old men that scared me. They would preach for what seemed like all day, talk loud, shout and stomp their feet, while walking up and down the aisle between the pews. I reckon that's why people call them "stomp down good preachers." The preacher I remember best was old Brother Lawhon. Although his sermons seemed to last all day, he was a mighty good preacher.

The Sundays I remember best were the ones when we had dinner on the grounds. Come to think of it, that's about what made church seem so long to me - sitting there thinking about that dinner we were fixing to have when the preacher finally got through. The Lord probably started

Sunday dinner on the grounds to make those of us that didn't like to go to church be there once in a while. One thing for sure, they ain't never made anything to match Sunday dinner on the grounds of the country church. Them good country women did know how to make food fitting to eat.

There's another thing, too, that took a big change on Sunday. That was the girls. The same little girl that looked ragged and spindly-legged at school during the week always looked plumb pretty at church on Sunday morning. A boy could nearly fall in love sitting there for a whole hour or two exchanging looks with some little girl. Of course, I always felt a little bit guilty about going back the next Sunday with nothing on my mind except looking at some little girl. Anyway, after dinner on the grounds, children usually played games around the church and in the school yard all afternoon while the old folks stood around the tables and caught up on the news. I tried to act big and listen to the men talk once in a while, but it never did amount to much to me. They were talking about somebody's meat getting skippers in it, or somebody's corn getting eaten by the weevils, Mr. So-and-So's milk cow losing a calf or his horse running away from home, and many such enlightening things as that , or so it seemed to me.

One of the things I can remember best is the big hickory trees that were so tall you could have climbed slam to the sky in some of them. The hickory nuts were so big they would bust your head it they hit you when they fell. They were fitting to eat, though, if you could ever get them out of the shell.

The stuff you needed if you were going to eat a hickory nut was a hammer, a brick, a bobby pin and six extra thumbs. You would take the hickory nut and put it on the brick and, while holding it so it couldn't fly off, hit it with the hammer. Sometimes you were lucky and busted the hickory nut instead of your thumb. That's when the bobby pin was used. You put it in the hand you held the hammer in because it still had a whole thumb on it. You picked the meat out of what little bit of shell that was not all smashed up. The ultimate torture in eating hickory nuts (we called them "hickor") comes when you got disgusted enough to quit trying to eat them and stepped barefoot on one of the shells. My advice to you is if you ever get hungry enough to eat hickory nuts, go find a pecan tree and settle for a bail of them. Hickory nuts were made for squirrels and those people you see who had teeth like they could eat corn off the cob through a picket fence. It seems like I'm always having to go back and clear things up, so let me go back and tell you now that hickory nuts grow on hickory tree like acorns grow on oak trees.

c. 1940 White Church Members

Back Row Left – W M Causseaux, Clifton Byrd, Bill Lawhon, Doyle Byrd, Wyche Byrd, ? TA Byrd, Artuur Wiggins, CK Causseaux, Clinton Spears, Walter Carroll, Lee Moody, Till Barrow, ?

Row 2 – Annie Browning, Maggie G Crosby, Eunice Carroll, Rawdon Crosby, Nora Causseaux, Ruby Lewis

Row 3 – Mary Benedict, Addie Wiggins, Mrs. C. Byrd, Spears Sister, Clara White, Therisia Scarbrough, Gwendolyn Spears, Maynard McDaniel, Bill Harris

Front Row 4 – Joanna Lewis, Sally Herring, Ruth Moody, Mrs. Alligood?, ?, Mrs. Moody, Mrs. Casey

Woodville School 1906-1942

SCHOOL DAYS <u>PG</u>

You may have noticed that I ain't said much about my school days. You can probably tell by now that it was not one of my favorite pastimes. Fact is, it fell pretty low down on the list of things to be about. However, with due force, Mamma talked me into starting school along about 1938. My first years were in the old two story frame building, about six or eight rooms that held all 12 grades.

I won't ever understand why I didn't like school, because I had a real good first grade teacher, in fact, she liked me so well that she kept me in first grade for two years. I kind of thought, though, that her reason for keeping me in her grade for two years was because she needed someone with experience to pass the word on to new students about what to do with the little specimen bottles that were sent home with us by the Health Department so we could be checked for hook worms. The thought of hook worms made me go look the subject up in the encyclopedia. And you know this is throwing a whole different light on my younger years. The encyclopedia says that some of the symptoms in children are a pale and pasty look, swollen abdomen, baggy eyes and dropsy in the legs. It also says he becomes lazy, indifferent and dull. Boy, I ain't never heard a better description for the children in my area in the late 1930s. Anyway, back to school - the best attendance record we had was by a real healthy hook worm.

When I started school we had 12 grades, but it dropped back to nine in about 1942. I managed to squeeze through the 9th grade after about eleven years. I feel better about it now though, that I know my failure was caused by a hook worm.

1942 School Operetta Vegetable Costumes Pete Gerrell 4th from Left. He is dressed as a tomato.

When I was about nine years old, a man came to the school and said that he wanted to start a local Scout troop. Any of us boys that were interested in joining the Boy Scouts should bring 50 cents to school so we could join. Naturally, I didn't have 50 cents, I didn't have 5 cents. So I came home and I asked Daddy about giving me 50 cents to join the Boy Scouts. That's where he used a little strong language again and he said,

"Son, I don't think you need to join the Boy Scouts, I'll teach you all you need to know about scouting." I didn't know how true that was. I never got the 50 cents, but he always talked about the 50 cents that I saved by not joining the Boy Scouts.

I learned other things from him. Well, one day we were riding in the woods and I saw several buzzards circling over an area. I said, "Daddy, what do you think those buzzards are circling over that area for?" He just said, "Shoot, son everything has gotta be somewhere."

It was almost as good as the chewing tobacco. I've never chewed tobacco but one time in my life. A boy brought some to school and one of the few times I went to school, he gave me a big plug of that tobacco at noon. We were out behind the Woodville School, close to the White Cemetery. We were out there on the edge of the cemetery and he cut me off a piece of that chewing tobacco. I had just eaten what little bit of lunch I had.

I chewed that tobacco and swallowed some of the juice. I started turning green and I spent most of the afternoon out there in that cemetery laying in the shade of a tree trying to get a hold of myself. I needed to go back to school or get home, so Momma wouldn't be wondering what had happened to me. I know that she knew when I got back to the house; sometime about 4:30 that evening. She knew something was wrong with me. I didn't ever tell her what. I still had all my chores to do. But that broke me. Three times during that afternoon in the cemetery I felt like 1 was probably in the right place. I was going to die anyway and I was in the cemetery, so all they'd have to do is just dig a hole and roll me over in it. Because, I was ready to go.

That brings up some other thoughts about school. You'll see where we say a lot of words like "hickor" instead of hickory and "cept" instead of except. I just never did see wasting time putting an ex in from of cept or all in front of most. You'd be surprised at how much talking time you saved by shortening your words like we do. When it comes to saying "those boys" instead of "tem boys" my old teacher taught me that I was supposed to say more when it didn't mean much more, like "almost every time" when "most every time" would do.

CHAPTER SIX

DAILY LIFE <u>PG</u>

Gathering firewood was always a constant chore. We used wood almost all of the time and kept a fire going somewhere, under the wash pot, making soap, cooking out lard, washing the clothes or whatever. Also, we had the fireplaces, those of us that were lucky enough to have a fireplace in the house. The hands usually had a place outside where they cooked but some of them were lucky enough to have a small wood stove in the house. We had gigging wood that we were always getting up. We would take the mule, hook him to the wagon, go through the woods and gather wood. In those days the hearts of old virgin pine timber that had died were there in abundance, so it was no problem to get plenty of fat lighter to burn. Also, we kept a supply of wood for the sugar kettle to make syrup and scald hogs. There was always a supply for the turpentine stills. We used pine wood in the stove to cook with. Daddy would mark a tree, usually one that was lightening struck. We would cut it down and cut it into about 12" blocks. The blocks would be split into small pieces to fit in the stove. The cutting was done with a 6 foot long crosscut saw and the block spitting with the ax. After the blocks were split the wood was stacked "hog pen style" at the wood pile outside the kitchen.

Speaking of washing the clothes, that was something that was done usually once a week on Mondays. There was a bench about waist high with two or three tubs of water placed on it. One of the tubs had a scrub board with soap in the water. The other two tubs had clear water in them for rinsing. The wash pot was nearby, far enough away that the heat from the fire wouldn't make you any hotter than you already were.

Incidentally, this whole set-up was usually located under a good big shade tree. It was also located near whatever the water supply was, whether it be the river, the spring, the pump or the open well. After washing, the clothes were hung out on lines to dry. Usually they were dry by late afternoon and could be brought in before the afternoon thunderstorms started moving through. This was usually a steady thing during the summer part of the year anyway. I have seen it get cold enough that the wet clothes would freeze on the clothesline. We would have to wait until the next day or possibly two or three days before we would have clean clothes to change into.

Shirts were made out of flour sacks and usually had about four buttons on them. The buttons were salvaged from an old shirt or pair of underwear that we had worn out. Grandmamma always kept a box of buttons that she'd salvaged from one thing or another. There were several different kinds of buttons that were used, even to pieces of oyster shells with holes drilled in them. Most of the clothes were handed down. Luckily, I was the oldest boy, so I usually got to wear the clothes first, and then my two younger brothers got them. The britches that I wore were usually store bought. We ordered from a catalog, Sears and Roebuck or Montgomery Wards. We had both of those catalogs and I'll tell you about the other uses for them in the outhouse later on.

Every family had two women that didn't live at home, a midwife and a washer woman. Our washer woman was old Aunt Lizzie. She wasn't really my aunt because she was the same color as the ice man. Lizzie came every Monday to wash clothes. My job on Monday morning was to fill the wash pot and the two wash tubs with water. Then I had to build a fire under the wash pot.

Aunt Lizzie would put the dirty clothes in the wash pot and boil them in soapy water. She didn't have a box of Tide or Cheer, so I'll tell you about the soap. If the soap was store bought it was Octagon soap. Octagon was the name brand, although it did come with eight sides. It was kind of a yellowish/orange color and was packaged in one pound bars. Sometimes we used homemade soap that was made from hog lard left over from last year, potash and lye mixed together. This was all put in the wash pot and boiled. I'll tell you, that stuff would flat clean a pot of clothes.

After the clothes were boiled, they were taken out and put into the wash tub to drain and cool. When they were cool enough they were moved to the wash tub with a scrub board in it and scrubbed. After a good scrubbing all over, with a few extra strokes on the knees and seat of the britches, they were moved to the rinse tub. After rinsing, they were hung on the line to dry.

You may wonder how I can remember the washer woman's name

so well and why I know so much about washing clothes. I'll tell you. The wash bench, the bench the tub sat on, was in the coolest place in the yard, under a big old chinaberry tree. Well, one fall day, Aunt Lizzie was doing her wash at the same time us boys needed some ammunition for our reed chinaberry guns. You had to climb the tree to get good chinaberries so I don't have to tell you who fell in Aunt Lizzie's wash tub. She got mad and left right in the middle of a week's wash.

I will always believe she and Mamma were in cahoots on that deal because she didn't show up the next Monday either. We had to do a whole week's wash. It taught us boys a real good lesson and I don't mean how to wash clothes either. We have always been real independent and a little hard headed. We don't generally beg for anything, but you'd better believe that we begged Aunt Lizzie to come back and be our washer woman again. She wouldn't answer us right off, left us seething for a week. I've never been more happy to see anybody in my whole life as I was to see that old black woman the next Monday morning as she came down the road to the house.

During the summer time we hardly ever wore shoes. We would go barefooted and save our shoes to wear during the winter. We did usually have an old hat that was passed down from Granddaddy or Daddy or one of the uncles that we could wear. It was usually too big for us, but it did shade our heads. The turpentine hands in the woods had basically the same kind of clothes, theirs were just more worn out than ours were and they usually had tar caked on them. They had to wear shoes because their feet were exposed to the elements and the things in the woods all the time. They wore a pair of old brogan type shoes, with what they called "leggins" that were laced up and made of either leather or canvas. They came up to just below their knees and protected the shin portion of their legs. These would be laced up on top of the pants legs.

Because of the bugs, mosquitoes, ticks, yellow flies, and other bugs, we had to drink sulfur water. This kept sulfur in our system to repel the bugs. Granddaddy had a pump on a big sulfur spring that was out in the river. When I say big, probably four or five feet across and running a pretty good stream of water all of the time. The sulfur coming out of it was so strong that as it ran down to the river it would turn the grass in the river yellow. A yellow coating would be on the river grass down below the spring for a hundred or two hundred feet. Granddaddy put a pump on the sulfur spring by putting a pipe with a filter and a foot valve down in the spring and then running the pipe to the pitcher pump out on the hill. We would pump the water from the old pitcher pump into a bucket and take it back to the house where it set on the shelf on the back porch, with the dipper.

Sulfur Spring on the St. Marks River

We would take powdered sulfur and put it in the cuff of our britches, in our shoes or just rub it into the britches legs to keep the ticks and bugs from crawling up our legs. Ticks were really bad. What they called "seed ticks", which were real small ones, would get on you by the thousands and you could hardly get them off. You couldn't wash them off. You had to get some alcohol or something to get them off. I would actually wash down in kerosene from the old kerosene lamp just to get the seed ticks off me. I remember one night I came home from fire hunting (I'll tell you about fire hunting later - it's hunting deer at night with a light.) I had gotten into a mess of these seed ticks and had them on me.

It was real cold and I didn't realize that I had them on me like that until I got to the house and climbed in bed. Dale and I slept in the same bed and that night he had gone to sleep on the wrong side, my side. After I went to sleep the ticks got warm and started to crawl. I started picking them off and dropping them on Dale. I thought I was dropping them on the floor. He shook me and woke me up and told me to quit putting those ticks on him, get out of bed and get them off. So I had to get up and take a bath in lye soap and cold water, it was probably about 25-30 degrees outside, but that was the only place we had to take a bath. Usually we took a bath in the sugar kettle down at the pond where we had fresh water, but it was a quarter of a mile away.

Another thing I need to tell you about is the outhouse. Ours was a two holer. I never did figure out whether it had two holes so two people could go at the same time, or whether you were supposed to alternate on using the holes so you would scatter the stuff out more and not have to dig it out so often.

I've seen them with square holes and triangular shaped holes, but ours had round holes. That's another thing I used to wonder about, too. Just what a person would look like from the rear after several years of using one of those things with triangular shaped holes. I just bet it would tend to have some effect on how a person looked going away from you. That may be something that would bear some research.

The outhouse was about five feet square with about a two foot by six foot door on the left front of it. The board that had the two holes in it went the full five feet across the back half and sat about two feet off the floor.

The front, below the boards with the holes in it, was enclosed and the rest of it was floored. When the door was closed, it was latched from the inside by string. One end of the string was fastened to the door permanently and the other would be wound around a nail on the side wall after you got in. The top, under the eaves, had vent holes in it. The wall boards had about quarter inch cracks in them so you could have plenty of ventilation, which you always needed. We didn't have toilet paper, but there was always plenty of old magazines and catalogs around. I don't ever remember a time when it was comfortable enough to stay in the outhouse and read. It was always too hot, too cold or smelled too bad. In the wintertime the wind coming across this half mile of open field to the northwest would almost make you cry. Come to think of it, that cold wind coupled with the smell would bring tears to your eyes anyway.

The outhouse always did look like a snaky place, which brings up the thought of the most shocking thing about one. That was when a chicken happened to get under it and reach up and peck you on the bottom. You could just see yourself laying up on some doctor's operating table, on your belly, while he treated you for a snake bite on the rear.

One of the worst whippings I ever got was caused by that string that held the door shut on the outhouse. It was Sunday afternoon and all the men were sitting on the back porch visiting. The back porch just naturally overlooked the barns, horse lot and the outhouse. One of my aunts, who was a pretty young thing back then, had gone to the outhouse. Some of the older young'uns, seeing the chance for a little fun, dared me to run by the outhouse and swing the door open.

I really didn't think that string would break, so I took the dare. Well, that string did break and there was my aunt, sitting up there on the throne, just as big as life, with all those men sitting on the back porch looking down at her. There I was, loping off down across the field, knowing that I was a dead goner. That run-by brought on several red faces and one awful red rear. One thing for sure, I'm glad we don't have outhouses anymore because it used to be that every time I'd see one, it would remind me of that whipping.

I'd best go back and make sure this outhouse business is cleared up before I start heading anywhere else. The reason I want to clear it up is because they were called so many different things. You know, there were a bunch of different outhouses on the farm. If you went by what some people called outhouses, some people called the barn, the chicken house the syrup house, the sugar house, crib and stables, all of them were outhouses. What we called the outhouse, though, was the place you went when you had to go.

When we were on the river at Grandma French's we would call it the "privy", because that's what she called it. Some people called theirs a "Johnny", but I never did know why. All the Johnnys I ever met were pretty good people, and I just couldn't see anybody naming that place after a person. Granddaddy used to say he couldn't see why people wanted to put the privy inside the house, close to where you cook and eat.

I think moving it inside though was the best thing that ever happened to mankind. A person would almost rather spend the night in a terrible strain than to go down to the outhouse when it was real cold and dark. Another thing, too, there wasn't any light in it so you never knew when someone else had the same problem you had. When you swung the door open, shaking scared already from the trip down there and the strain you were just naturally under because you had waited so long, and somebody spoke up from the dark dungeon. Buddy, it was just "pass the catalog" then.

Grandma kind of beat the business of going outside at night, though. She had what was called a "slop jar" that was a white porcelain bucket that was about as big as a water bucket and had a lid on it. She kept it under the edge of the bed, so if you really got in a pinch you could borrow her slop jar. One thing a slop jar did was make you question Grandma's love for you. You could really get some doubts about it when she asked you to take the slop jar out and empty it.

MAMA'S COOKING

My brother and I get together at my mother's house now. She is in her mid 80s and she still likes to fix lunch for us, so we get together there once a week and have lunch with her and talk about the old times. She used to make all of our clothes and she also kept plenty of good food cooked and on the table in our early years. Her table was usually the main attraction. She always kept a sheet spread over it with something under the sheet. Mamma didn't have to tell us to stay out of the refrigerator because, as I've told you, we didn't have one. All of the

Pecan Pound Cake

3 Sticks softened Butter
6 oz. buttermilk
2 tsp vanilla
3 Cups Plain Flour
3 Cups Sugar
6 Eggs (Add 1 at a time)

1 Cup Chopped Pecans

Preheat oven to 325. Cream Butter & sugar, Add Buttermilk, (mix with mixer) Add vanilla, (Mix) Add 3 cups plain flour (mix with mixer 1 cup at a time), Eggs should be at room temperature. Add one at a time and mix. Mix all ingredients together for 4 minutes at medium speed. Add chopped nuts with spoon. Bake 1 hour 45 minutes.
Jessie Gerrell

leftover food was on the table under the sheet. There was also cornbread, biscuits or both, bacon or homemade sausage. One of my favorite after school snacks was corn bread crumbled up in a bowl of fresh milk.

Another one of my favorites was cracklin' bread. Boy, Mamma knew how to cook that stuff. **Cracklin' bread** was regular corn bread with the cracklins cooked in with it. For those of you who don't know what **cracklins** are, I'll tell you. During hog killing, the fat was trimmed from the pork. This fat was cut into small pieces and put in the wash pot. When the wash pot was filled with fat trimmings consisting of pieces with and without skin on them, a slow fire was built under the wash pot. The fire was kept burning for four or five hours, until all the lard was cooked out of the fat. It had to be stirred every few minutes while cooking. The stirring was done with a flat hickory paddle about two inches wide and about three feet long. When most of the pieces floated to the top, you knew that the lard was done. The pieces would turn light brown and crispy while cooking. The lard was then poured into 25 pound lard cans and the cracklin's were strained out of it. The lard, which was used for frying foods, was stored in the smokehouse. The cracklins were stored in crocks to be used in cracklin' bread. The only problem with cracklins was that we never had enough to last all year.

Just to give you an example of Mamma's cooking, I'll tell you about greens. If some of the stuff I'm telling you about doesn't sound good, it is because you don't eat it from Mamma's table. Greens are turnip or mustard, fresh out of the garden, cooked on a wood stove, seasoned with a piece of cured side meat I told you about. It seems like they had to cook all day because of the length of time I had to smell them cooking before I could eat some. The smell of that cornbread baking in the oven didn't do my belly no harm either. When I finally did get seated before a big plate of those greens, all I could do is say, "Mamma, pass me some more." Not only were the greens and the cornbread good, but that pot liquor just took a boy's heart away. Pot liquor is the juice the greens were cooked in. After eating all the greens I could hold, I crumbled a piece of cornbread up in a cup of pot liquor and would go some more. You know, I may just have to go see Mamma after I finish writing this and let her cook me some more.

Working in the woods with the livestock and the turpentine trees, doing all the things that we had to do to maintain 800 head of cattle and several hundred head of hogs and take care of the land that we had, we would usually eat a hog or a cow a week. Usually in the winter we ate wild game. The old cows were not very big anyway; they were small range cows, longhorns. Usually the pork or beef would be cooked in the simplest forms.

Another thing she definitely knew how to cook was venison hash. She would cook that stuff down to a low gravy, put it on the table with a bowl of grits and a big plate of buttermilk biscuits and, buddy, if you didn't sit up and take notice something was definitely wrong with you, especially thinking about that homemade syrup you were going to pour over two more of those biscuits when you finished your grits and venison gravy.

Slumgullion

Meat – Use ground meat, sausage, or pulled meat. Whatever kind you like or have
Corn
Tomatoes
Onion – if you have it
Peas
Potatoes chopped – if you have them
If you have other leftovers that will mix, throw them in. Add water.
Season to taste.

In the 1930's with money scarce and some foods rationed, cooks got inventive with what they had. Jessie Gerrell used this recipe. It was probably never exactly the same. It varied by what she had available. The end result was a thick soup or thin stew that would feed many people.

TG

    Jessie French Gerrell was an amazing woman, a true southern matriarch. She almost always had a smile and a hug and yet she could in some ways rule the family with a gentle suggestion. This section would not be complete without some of her memories. She is not here to tell them for us but her daughter, Marilee Gerrell Butler has written a piece that mentions some of Jessie's favorite memories. It follows.

Jessie French c. 1925

JESSIE'S MEMORIES

This family belonging to Walter and Jessie French Gerrell is a family of storytellers. The older we get, the more precious become these memories, these stories of our family, our growing up together in a very family-oriented time and place, and our loss of some of these precious souls who have gone on before us.

Meeting weekly at our favorite restaurant (usually seafood), the Gerrells- Marilee Butler, Terri (Pete's widow), Dale and Dee, Lawson and Jadon- reminisce about old times. Reminiscing is, according to the dictionary, "remembering one's past" or "a recollection narrated or told." These Gerrells are past masters of this art! Pete used this method of the "three Rs"~ rambling, reminiscing, and repeating-in his books, <u>Old Trees</u> and <u>The Illustrated History of the Naval Stores Industry.</u>

Our mother, Jessie French Gerrell (1910-2002), had many stories of growing up "over the (St. Marks) river", southeast of Natural Bridge. Many of her stories have become legend to our family. As we would drive through the gate of Gerrell Plantation, once the home and lands of her father, James Roston French, Jessie would click out of her seatbelt. Now she was home. Almost every bend in the sandy road would remind her of a family story.

Many years before, her father had a mailbox at the entrance to his property. Some of his descendants have their mailboxes there now. Jessie would remember the French family receiving their mail, which included newspapers, magazines, periodicals, letters, and other reading materials. After supper, the entire family-Jim, Mollie, Elsie, Ina, Frank, Jessie, and baby Nina (she probably read the funnies) would gather on the spacious back porch. After a time of reading, family members would discuss what they had read. Jessie's favorite was <u>Ranch Romances</u>. There were always books in the French home and Jim had many books on the law. Jessie remembered her father's desk-a square table with a gas lamp for reading in the "front room." Jim's law books were in a bookcase near his desk and they were off-limits to the grandchildren! Jim was well respected in the political and financial arenas in Leon and Wakulla Counties.

As we crossed the cattlegap into the "pasture", as the Plantation was often called, Jessie would be reminded of the "river cows" owned by her father and later her husband, Walter Gerrell. These cows fed on underwater grass in the St. Marks River. In 1952, a Jacksonville newspaper had an article about the cows grazing in the river, ducking their heads underwater to feed on the crisp, nutritious grass as the river water cooled them and kept flies off them. What a cow's life! So inbred were the cows that their distinctive markings were passed down through the years.

A big decision as we drove in was whether to travel left on the Schoolhouse Road or continue south on Jim French Road. Usually we would choose Schoolhouse Road, passing the Burns Place, where Jessie's father was born in 1869 to James Whaley and Emmaree Duggar French. The Burns Place was the site of the staging area during the Battle of Natural Bridge.

The Schoolhouse Road is so named because it led to the area's one-room schoolhouse, described by Pete Gerrell in <u>Some Wakulla County Schools</u>. Pete (1932-2007) gleaned information about the Pinhook School from his mother, Jessie, who was a pupil there from

1916 to 1920. Pete's essay on the schoolhouse can be found in <u>A Book of Halls</u> by his sister, Marilee Gerrell Butler.

From the Schoolhouse Road, we turned south to the Hall Cemetery where six generations of Halls and their descendants are buried. Elizabeth Byrd Hall, widow of Enoch Hall of Appling County, Georgia, had brought her seven children to this area before 1830. Elizabeth's son, Lewis Hall, homesteaded to the south of the cemetery and Lewis' son, Lewis Franklin established his home to the east of the cemetery on land that Terri and Pete now own. Pete found many artifacts in these homesteads and others. Pete is buried in the Hall Cemetery under his "tomb stump." Four Confederate soldiers are buried here and another, who is buried at Magnolia Cemetery, has a memorial stone here.

Leaving the Hall Cemetery, we glanced eastward toward the Booger Pond and Jessie shared another memory. Jessie remembered taking fresh water in a bucket to her daddy and having to pass by the Booger Pond. Jim's cows came rushing out of the pond and scared little Jessie. She climbed a pine tree. Bark from the tree fell into the bucket and when Jim asked her why there was bark in the water, she told him that there were boogers in the pond and the cows and the boogers scared her. Thus the name Booger Pond.

Continuing on our way south, we saw a place that instantly reminded Jessie of a prank played by her older sister, Frank. The site once held a house where the inhabitants had died, probably from typhoid fever or diphtheria. Jim French had warned his girls "not to go in through the door." Frank, being the smarty daredevil that she always was, proceeded to climb in through the window. She didn't disobey her father; she went in through the window, not the door.

Back on Jim French Road, Jessie looked for honeysuckle and cowslip along the roadside. In February she would see the violets that she loved so much coming up through the wiregrass. As we passed the sheep lot, she remembered Jim's 800- plus sheep and shearing time. The "big girls", Ina and Frank held the sheep down while Jim sheared.

As we drove south on Jim French Road, Jessie reminded us that this was the Pinhook Road that had led from the old town of Magnolia on the St. Marks River through the Pinhook area, which included the homes of Halls, Moores, Bums, Faircloths and others of our kin. The road continued on through Wacissa into South Georgia. It was also the road on which Jessie's older sisters walked south from their home to

Newport, where they were tutored by a teacher named Karl. They boarded with the Karl family and walked home on weekends. The Karls' were of German descent.

Now we were back at "The Cottage" which Jessie and Walter built on the site of Jim's and Mollie's "New House." After Walter died, Jessie and Marilee often spent the night at "The Cottage." Oftentimes on a moonlit night, Jessie would be sitting up at midnight watching for wildlife to cross the yard. Once we heard a rustling in the leaves and we saw two otters slithering across the yard chasing each other, heading toward the river.

As we left on our way home and went through the oak grove on Jim French Road, Jessie was reminded of the Tram Road that ran east from Vereen to Delph (now Fanlew) to the turpentine camp. She would recall that two men got off the tram at Dale's Fault in the oak grove. One of the men died and was buried there. The other man continued on to Delph. Jessie said that no one knew who the men were or where they had come from.

As we drove out of the gate on our way home, Jessie would click her seatbelt back on. Ah, well, back to the real world.

But, oh, the memories.

Submitted & written by: Marilee Gerrell Butler as told to her by Jessie French Gerrell

Ancient Live Oaks on the edge of the Booger Pond

Jessie French Gerrell in her 80s with her Great Grandson

CHAPTER SEVEN

FARMING: CLEARING LAND   <u>TG</u>

Clearing the land for use in Wakulla and Leon counties was not an easy task. It took hard labor and it did not happen overnight. It happened over months and years. Today if you want 5 acres cleared, you go in with a tractor, a root rake, something to pull up tree stumps and a very strong back. If luck is with you, in a couple of days you have 5 acres of cleared plowed land.

Now time travel back to the 1800s and even as late as 1950. The land was rough. Northwest Florida is full of large trees, briars, vines, scrub, low bush acorns, and I could go on and on with a list of lush vegetation. You get the picture. Florida was thick and overgrown and not always easy to tame. Dale Gerrell has described how his family cleared the land. Dale, Pete, and Lawson are all sixth generation Floridians that were following the successful practices of their early ancestors.

The land had to be cleared in small patches. Today we can clear large acreage with modern equipment. During the 1930-1950s the Gerrells cleared 2 acres per year. It was a labor intensive process.

At the beginning of each new year the new 2 acre plot to be cleared was taken in and fenced. This 2 acres was used to pen the Mama cows and their calves at night. As many as a hundred head of Mama cows would be in that two acre pen. The cows ate some of the vegetation and more importantly they fertilized it. It was not as easy to buy fertilizer back then as it is now. During the day the Mama cows were released to graze. This was before the FENCE law came into effect. The calves were left in the 2 acre pen. At night the Mamas were glad to come home and feed their babies. Throughout the year the Gerrell boys worked on clearing the land, cutting trees and getting rid of stumps. The stumps were set on fire daily and the smoke helped clear the area of bugs that affected both the cows and the family. Every 2 weeks the land was turn plowed. That means a plow pulled by a horse or mule and followed & guided by a person, most likely a Gerrell boy.

With perseverance, sore backs, and luck, the land was ready to be plowed by the end of the year. So now we have a new, very well fertilized 2 acre plot of land. The land was planted in a specific rotation.

The first crop in the first year this plot was used was the general family garden. A bit of many things good was grown.

Crop 2, the plot was used for sweet potatoes and melon.

Crop 3, the plot was used for sugar cane. A very important crop because it was a major source of affordable sweetener for cooking and income through the year. Cane would be grown in this plot for maybe 3-5 years until it got to thick to make a good crop

Crop 4, the field was used for velvet beans, field corn, peanuts, and chufa. Some of these were crops were used as animal feed.

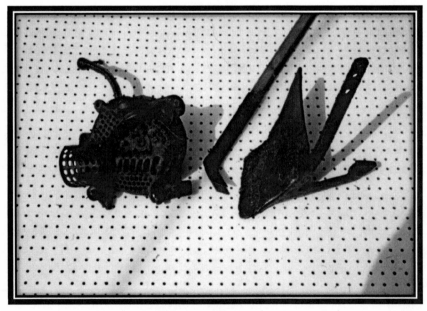

Common farm tools

Corn husker, cane stripper & plow blade.

FARM STORIES <u>PG</u>

When the war came on we moved back to the farm. Granddaddy Gerrell died and Daddy decided he wanted to go back to the farm and start farming. He had been running a meat market in Tallahassee. He wanted to go back to the farm and start farming and that way he wouldn't have to go into the military and serve in the war. We moved back to Grandma and Granddaddy Gerrell's house about three miles into the piney woods.

> Walter Gerrell was the sole support for his family of six and two elderly mothers. Farmers who were the sole supporters of large families were exempt from military service.

We sure enough moved in with a mess of work too. It was February when we moved back, so if we were going to get a crop in the ground that year, we had to shake a leg (for you all that don't know the meaning of "shake a leg", it means the same thing as light a shuck or get a move on).

The first tool Daddy introduced me to was a grubbing hoe. It was built sort of like an ace on one side and like a hoe on the other. The grubbing hoe was used to grub persimmon and sassafras bushes, which we had a whole heap of. The first field Daddy put me in looked like it was at least four miles square; although he said it only had twenty acres in it. One thing was for sure, it had enough bushes that I'd know how to use that grubbing hoe by the time I got through.

I always thought of hickory trees as being real tall. Well after three hours in that field, those persimmon and sassafras bushes looked to be the same size as hickory trees. The bushes had to be dug down deep enough that the point of the Dixie Boy plow wouldn't catch on them. I'll tell you about the old Dixie Boy plow later.

After four days in that field, I had flat fell in love with that grubbing hoe. We just always seemed to be alone together and I couldn't find a thing we had in common. It was a real marriage type true love. I finally got up the nerve to ask Daddy if that field had ever been broken up before or was it new ground? Daddy said, "Sure it was broke up before, boy. You see that hill over yonder? Well I was plowing on it in 1932, just before you were born, when the house caught on fire and burned." I didn't tell him, but, I couldn't see the hill for the bushes. The time just about fit too. Those bushes had about a ten year head start on me.

I don't remember ever getting through grubbing the bushes out of that field, but I must have because Daddy made his next introduction, the turn plow. I had played around the plows under the shed beside the old log crib long enough to know that I wasn't big enough to hold that thing up. What I didn't know was that the plow wasn't like a grubbing hoe. It had a working partner that went along with it and, of course, I had met him. He was that stubborn devil that lived in the horse lot, but didn't look like a horse. I was a little bit hard headed. When I say a little bit, I was comparing myself to that old mule. That mules' head was harder than the root on a ten year old persimmon bush and buddy, you'd better believe that's tough.

I'd better go back to getting the mule out of the lot, getting him decked out in all of that gear. He was always real hard to catch and I can sure understand why. After we finally did catch him, he was muzzled, blinded, gagged, choked and then tied with ropes and chains. After seeing him getting hitched up and ready to plow, I could understand why he was stubborn. After you got the trace chains, which went up and hooked on to the mule's collar and hooked to the singletree on the plow, you held on to the plow lines and let the mule drag the plow through the field.

I'd better tell you what plow lines are before we go any further so we'll be straight on that. Plow lines are the power

steering and brakes on a plow mule. You are supposed to holler "Gee" for him to turn right, "Haw" for him to turn left and "Whoa" for him to stop. I think all that hollering is just to help you hold your temper. A mule never did learn to understand people hollering, because he had his own special holler that he did. Man, he could sound off to another mule in the fields. No, I can't put in writing here how far a country mile is, but maybe you can ask me sometime. This old mule could be heard a country mile away.

Back to the plow lines; if you really wanted to make a mule turn right, you would pull the right plow line. Pulling the left line would make him turn left. Pulling both of them at the same time would make him stop. The reason the mule would turn and stop when you pulled the plow lines was because they were hooked to the bits which were run through the mule's mouth. Daddy said that bit didn't hurt a mule's mouth, but I really bet he had never put a set in his mouth to see if they hurt or not.

After getting the mule all hooked up and out to the field, I could understand why farmers had to get up so early and work so late. The first furrow through the field was not next to the fence, so Daddy went to the other end of the field and hung a white flag on a post. Then he came back and asked me if I could see it. I thought to myself, yeah, I can see it; they've raised the white flag down yonder and want to surrender. Why can't we do the same thing and all of us go home?

He told me I was supposed to aim the mule at the flag and try to go in a straight line to it. You have seen where a black snake has crawled across the dry sand. That's the way that furrow I plowed looked, real shallow and a whole lot crooked. Another thing was when you pulled on both the lines to make the mule stop; you needed a third hand to keep the plow from falling over. Daddy finally got disgusted enough at me that he made the first few rounds for me, and then he gave the lines back to me.

Me and that old mule would go round and round. We nearly had the same kind of love as I had with that grubbing hoe. The only thing was, when I got to one of them persimmon stumps that I hadn't cut down deep enough, the plow would jump over into the furrow it just plowed. When that happened, I would have to make the mule back up so I could start over, because the dirt was supposed to be turning over and covering up the furrow I had made on the last round. To make the mule back up I had to holler two words that nobody but the mule could understand. Those words sounded like "hack hear," which was supposed to be "back here" in people talk. After I got about half through, I got to thinking about those circles I was making around that field. Daddy was always telling me when I did something wrong that if I didn't straighten up we were going to go round and round. Those words sure did take on a meaning to me after that.

You know, there was another thing that I took a terrible disliking to while I was plowing. That was hogs. Granddaddy had planted chufa in the field before and then turned the hogs in on them. Chufas are a little nut that grows on a bush underground, like a peanut, only it doesn't have a shell like a peanut. They must grow awfully deep, maybe nearly to China, because some of the holes dug by those long-nosed hogs, old piney wood rooters, were deep enough to hide a Model A Ford in. Those holes sure did make for some bad trips with a mule and a turn plow.

After we got the field broken up good and the ground ready to plant, we took the **guano** distributor and put the fertilizer down. The fertilizer wasn't spread all over the field like it is today; it was just put down in the row where the seeds were going to be planted. The guano distributor was a wood box that sat on top of a stand. The stand was built sort of like a wheelbarrow frame with a wheel on the back of it. The box that held the fertilizer was built so it would roll like a rocking horse on the stand. As it rocked, a hole opened and closed in the bottom to let the fertilizer out. Guano was bird manure, fertilizer that was shipped in from South America.

That great piece of machinery was also operated by mule power, with some poor man walking behind it,

Our $4.35 Cotton Planter.

This is a perfect, reliable and very desirable cotton planter, and one which has had a tremendous sale in the great cotton belt of the south. It is made of first class materials throughout, has a large hopper, a splendid agitator and a perfect feed regulating device. Center shovel is strong and cannot break. Driving wheel is made of wood, 16 inches in diameter, 3 inches thick and beveled to run in the trench made by the shovel. The coverer is supported by steel springs, which allows it to adjust itself to the condition of the ground and relieves the hands of all jarring. This machine is also a first class fertilizer distributor as well as a cotton planter, requiring no extra parts, and by adding the corn planting attachment it makes a splendid corn drill, dropping the kernels about 24 inches apart. Shipped direct from factory in Southwestern Ohio.
No. 32R512 Cotton Planter only. Weight, 65 pounds. Price...................................$4.35
No. 32R513 Corn Planting Attachment extra. Weight, 5 pounds. Price...........................80c

We can always furnish repairs for our Implements at any time at the lowest prices. See notice on first page of this department.

doing about seven different jobs at one time. The man had to keep the distributor balanced when it was already top heavy because of the box sitting on top of it. He had to make sure it was shaking right and didn't get stopped up or put out too much fertilizer. The worst and biggest thing he had to do was the four operations it took to keep the mule straight and moving.

You know, I've done a lot of figuring in my day, but I've never figured out yet why anybody would want to be a farmer. Fishing or hunting are more like what I'm suited for. The poor old farmer has to work with and for the dumbest kind. I say poor and old because most farmers are poor and all of them look old. They worked with a dumb, stupid mule all summer to make food to feed him all winter so he will be able to work the next summer. Come to think of it, maybe that mule isn't so dumb and stupid as I might think. He's the one that gets to stand around all winter and do nothing but eat the food that was made in the summer. Another thing, too, he didn't have to try to figure any answers for all the mess you get from the government.

The next thing I'll tell you about is the planter. It was built sort of like the distributor, except it had two boxes sitting on it, side by side. Instead of shaking the seeds out, it had plates in the boxes that turned round and round. The plates had little notches in them that the seeds fell into when the notch went down to the bottom of the box. When the notch got to the top of the box, the seed fell through a little hole and into the furrow that a plow on the front of the planter was opening. There were two plows on the back of the planter, right behind the wheel that was pulling the dirt back into the furrow and covering up the seeds.

The reason for two boxes was so you could plant two different kinds of seeds at one time. We usually planted peas and corn in the same row. The plates came with different sized notches and some had notches closer together than others. By putting in a plate with bigger holes, you could plant more seeds to the hill. By putting in a plate with more holes, you could plant seeds closer together. You see, I told you that thing was a high class piece of machinery. Another thing, too, you never went to use a planter that you didn't have to change the plates. We had about eight or ten different sized plates that hung on a nails in the barn. Choosing which one to use took a lot of deciding.

By the time you got the seeds in the ground you can see, a heap of work had gone on. You could kind of see a comparison between the mule and the farmer beginning to come on. Both of them had their ribs showing and were looking old. Last year's corn was getting low in the crib so it was being rationed out a little slower. Now, the farmer and the mule were on double work and half rations.

WINDMILL DREAMS   <u>PG</u>

We had a windmill pump to water our horses but it did not have a windmill. It was hand operated. I did not really know how much water the average horse's intestines and stomach could hold until I started research for this book. Come to find out, my suspicions were right; a horse could drink 220 quarts or over a barrel of water. Guess that's why Old Slogans spent many nights without enough water. Good thing he wasn't an ox though, the average ox holds 337 quarts or about two barrels of water.

Talking about the horse lot reminds me that the first place I ever saw real running water (no I'm not fixing to say what you think I am) was a pipe we had that ran about a hundred feet into the horses trough. I'll tell you how it was. First we had the windmill pump that was on the back porch at the house. Under the spout of the windmill pump we had a cypress board box that held about 20 gallons of water. The pipe to the horse lot ran from the bottom of the box to a busted 80 gallon sugar kettle that acted as a horse trough. I told you that I was going to tell you about windmills and I bet you think I'm fixing to get off on that now. Well, I'm not, because our windmill pump didn't have a windmill.

It had to be worked by hand. Usually when I pumped water for

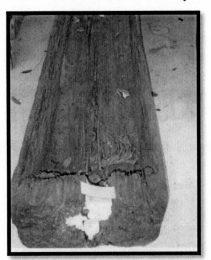

the horse I would stick an old rag in the pipe while I was pumping. That way it would look like I was making some headway. After I got the box full, I'd pull the rag out and let the water run to the horses. I bet you have never stopped to think about how much water four horses and a big mule could drink. Them things would stand there drinking for what seemed like forty forevers before they would get full. After they got full, the trough still had to be left full. There is one thing I did an awful lot of thinking on, how to steal the neighbors' windmill. I just could never figure how to hide it and still get it to the pump. I guess it could have been worse, though. Daddy had to draw water out of an open well with a bucket when he was young. He never told me so, but I'll bet those horses when to sleep thirsty a bunch of nights back in those days.

That old windmill pump was something else. It could out pump a pitcher pump three to one. It even had the shaft running out of the top so all you had to do is hook the windmill on it. Man, I dreamed a bunch of times there was a windmill over that thing, just turning along in the breeze, jugging up and down with the clear, cool, water pouring freely from the spout. I didn't stop to think about it, but now that I mention it, I'll bet the horses and that old mule had the same dream a bunch of times, too.

Talking about the open well, when we are eating lunch with Mamma, my brothers and I get to talking about things and Mamma just shakes her head and says, "I don't know how you boys ever got grown." She never says, "I don't know how I ever raised you." The open well reminds me of the time when a neighbor boy got spinal meningitis. I had been playing with him a couple of days before he was diagnosed with it. Mamma was real concerned that I would get spinal meningitis from the boy. She didn't really know that in our playing we had been playing in an old abandoned open well that was about fifteen feet deep and the weeds had grown up around it. It had already started caving in around the sides. Spinal meningitis from another kid was not necessarily the only threat to life that we had.

PG

One of the things that Momma usually kept on the table was sweet potatoes. Most the time they were just baked in the oven and put on the table. You had to peel it to eat it. I don't care anything for them now and that's probably for several reasons. First, the process of planting and harvesting them. The planting was called "sticking the draws'" which was done by sticking a potato draw in the newly plowed ground with a stick. The potato draw was a piece of vine that was taken off of a growing vine. The stick that was used was about three feet long, with a notch carved in the bottom end of it. The potato draw was placed under the notch and pushed in a hole in the ground. You then used your heel to mash the dirt in tight around the potato draw and make a hole for watering. Watering was the next thing that turned me against sweet potatoes. They always had to be planted the furthest from the pump so we'd have more of a distance to tote the water. Remember, there were no electric pumps and no garden hoses. We had a pitcher pump that we used to pump water into a foot tub. A foot tub is built about twice as wide as a water bucket so you can get more bruises on your legs and spill more water on your long trip across the hot field. What little bit of water that is left in the foot tub when you get to the potato patch is poured on the potato draws with a metal dipper.

The next thing that makes me wild about sweet potatoes is that you have to dig them. I won't even explain that nasty back braking job. Next is to bank the potatoes. A potato bank is a lean-to built on the ground. The back is in the ground and the front is about four feet above the ground. The potatoes are put into the bank in layers. A layer of dried pine straw is put down, then a layer of potatoes, a layer of pine straw, and then another layer of potatoes on top of it. (and on, and on) This is an operation you do while bending down and kneeling. When you get ready to cook them you dig them up, enough for a meal. Again, you are bent over and kneeling. It is for sure you don't have to bless the sweet potatoes before eating them. They've been prayed over enough.

TG

(In all the years I spent with my husband, the only time I saw him voluntarily eat a sweet potato was when we were dating and he fried some Sweet Potato French fries to show me how good they could really be. I had told him the week before that I liked sweet potatoes.)

I was telling you about the sweet potatoes. The tomatoes were almost as bad. They had to be set out as plants and watered with water from the pond or from the pitcher pump. Naturally, they were set out on the far side of the field somewhere, where you had to carry the water in the old foot tub all the way across the field, bouncing it off your legs. The only thing was, when you picked the tomatoes you didn't have to bank them in banks and dig them up a second time.

One of the things that Daddy told me about that I kind of wondered about, was that he said if I started lifting the old milk cow's calf over the fence when it was born and do that every day, I could still lift it over the fence when it got grown. I never stopped to think about it, but that may be why I have back problems now.

Talking about the milk cow brings up another whole bunch of thoughts. I guess I'd better start at the front of this and go through the whole thing with you. Milking a cow by hand is about as far gone as plowing with a mule. Speaking of plowing with a mule, you see how good I am at staying away from it. We had several milk cows after I got old enough to milk, that I could call by name. Some of the names that I called them wouldn't do to put in writing. Another thing, too, I use the name milk cow kind of loosely. Some of those bones and hides that we milked were just plain old range cows. Instead of measuring the milk they gave by the gallon, we measure it by the cup. The only cow that I can remember milking that was half decent was a jersey that Daddy bought. She would give about a gallon and a half twice a day and still have enough left for her calf.

I don't even remember learning how to milk a cow; it was just something that the calf and I always knew. He would get on the left side and I would get on the right and we would race to see who could get the mostest the fastest. Nearly every time we got together, which was twice a day, one of us would touch a place on the old cow's tit that had been snagged by briars and somebody would get kicked. As long as she had her head in the feed bucket she would stand fairly still, but when she got through eating you'd better get out of the way or get ready to be stepped on.

It took three buckets for me to milk that old jersey. One had feed for her to eat while I milked. One was empty, which I used to sit on while I milked. The other one had warm water in it that I used to wash her bag. After her bag was washed, the water that was left would be thrown out. Then the milk was put in that bucket. Everyone had his own was of squeezing a cow's tit to get the milk out of it. My way was to press the back of my thumb to the tit, then wrap my fingers around and squeeze. What looked real funny was to see a group of old country boys comparing their various ways of milking, especially if you couldn't hear what they were saying. You didn't know whether they were going to hit, slap or just threaten each other.

I was telling you about the milk cows, but I didn't tell you about keeping the milk afterwards. After you got the milk, since we didn't have refrigerators to put it in, we would put it in a milk house down at the edge of the river swamp, which was under a big live oak tree in a real cool place. Also, we would take it and put it in quart jars, seal it and put it down in the springs where we got our water from. It was a flowing sulfur spring that was actually up on the hill. It wasn't the Seminole Spring down in the river that I told you about.

Sulfur Spring at River Used for Storing Butter & Milk

The Spring is cooler than the River which is always at a temp of low 70's or below. This offered a way of keeping things cool in days past.

Forty years after the last cow was milked there at that house, in the mid 1990s, we were digging out the spring. (We still have a house there and Mamma likes to go down and get a drink of sulfur water) We dug up a bottle of butter that had been there for forty years under the water. You could still tell what it was. It was still the color of butter until we opened it and then it turned black almost immediately. It had been forty years since any butter had been put in the spring.

Dale was milking the cow one time and she kept swinging her tail around and hitting him on the side of the head. He took the cow's tail and tied it to the gate by the hair on the end of the tail. The old cow got ready to go after she finished eating. She just started to walk off and

Dale got up to jump out of her way. When he did, it scared the cow and she ran. She pulled the end of her tail off. When Daddy saw what Dale had done he used some pretty strong language about it and told Dale that he should make him walk around with a limb keeping the flies whipped off that cow's back until her tail grew back. The poor cow's tail never did grow any hair back on it, but he put a sack on it and kept it oiled and it did heal up.

When I say we didn't make any money off the farm, that's mainly because we had to feed that blasted mule or put a little bit of food on our table. We farmed in poor white sand and it was covered with briars and sand spurs. You can see why we probably didn't make anything, trying to fertilize it with bird manure out of South America somewhere. There were some years that we planted corn that we thought we were going to have to dig it instead of just break it. What we did have was what was called "nubbin corn", little small ears. Throw it in the crib and just hold it up for the mule. That old log crib that we kept the corn in had holes in the sides of it, between the logs. The rats would live in there and we would take a .22 rifle and shoot the rats. One time we took an old light wood knot out of the woods and it was so crooked we threw it in the corn crib with the corn. It shucked and shelled all the corn during the night and crawled out between a crack in the logs and was gone the next morning.

We had an old boy that lived to the west of us that rode a mule. In the evenings, after he would come in from school, he would want to come down and play with us. About halfway between the two houses, which was about a quarter of a mile, there was an old black stump. We noticed that old mule would always shy around that black stump. One evening, I went down and hid behind the black stump and when the mule got there and started to shy around it, I jumped up and hollered. When I did the mule went home. Needless to say, the boy wasn't on the mule. It took him a little while to get up and shake the sad off so he could go home. It was several days before he came back to see us to play again, and when he did, he didn't ride by the old black stump.

I told you about old big boy and him dying with an unknown disease. I had gone to see him before he died. I guess if Mamma had known I had gone into that house with that old big black fellow and him with his skin busting open, she would have probably took me apart for that. Anyway, we had another old turpentine hand that lived on the other side of us from where Big Boy did, his name was Dexter. His wife's name was Maggie.

Old Dex would work around the farm. He had gotten too old to work in the turpentine woods. Maggie just kept house. They lived in a little one room house with a kitchen on the back of it that had been there for probably 100 or 125 years. I was going by Dexter and Maggie's house one time and I noticed Maggie was out in the yard working with a fire. Incidentally, Dexter liked to trap rabbits, coons, possums and things like that to eat. He would trap them and occasionally trap a skunk and get into that, too. Maggie was cooking something so I asked her what she was cooking. She said she was cooking possum and taters, that she had put the possum wrapped in a wet rag or cloth under the ashes the night before, along with some sweet potatoes and she just kept the hot ashes over the possum and potatoes all night. When I got there the next day and asked her what she was doing, she invited me in to try some of it. I didn't really care for the sweet potatoes anyway, but I did eat some of the possum and it was almost like eating fat pork.

Sweet Potato Casserole/Soufflé

4 c. mashed sweet potatoes
2 eggs
1 tsp vanilla
½ c. milk
½ c. brown sugar
½ c. white sugar

Topping;
2/3 c. brown sugar
1/3 c. butter or margarine
¾ - 1 c. chopped pecans
1/3 c. flour

Mix top 6 together and place in a baking dish. For topping, mix sugar, flours and margarine cutting with a fork. Add chopped pecans to make a crumble. Sprinkle over potatoes and bake at 350 degrees for 35-40 minutes. Terri Gerrell

---

CHAPTER EIGHT

CATTLE

FENCE <u>TG</u>

In Florida prior to 1949, farm animals such as cattle and hogs were permitted to run free. Ownership was proved and determined by marking and branding the animals. Over time this became an issue. Populations were growing and automobiles were becoming widely used. If an animal moved onto a road or near it there could be problems.

Cattle Ranging In the Piney Woods

<u>PG</u>

Since the beginning of time, man has made his barriers from natural materials adjacent to the barrier sight. These materials were mostly wood from trees, stone, thorny brush, and soil. The art of making wire dates back to about 400 A.D. Hot bloom iron was pulled through dies in a drawing plate which produced short lengths of smooth wire.

Man tried to use smooth wire to enclose livestock but found that it was not a dependable deterrent.

The Florida Legislature decided to activate the Florida Fence Law in 1949. It required that all cattle be fenced off the roads. We had cattle that ranged all over in the open woods. My granddaddies had bought the cattle as the earlier settlers moved out and left the old farmed out lands. They sold their cows to one or the other of my granddaddies so we had the Jones cows, the Smith cows, and the Hall cows. The cows would always stay within the same area where they had been raised.

TG

The Gerrell family knew about the coming change two years before the law came into effect. Walter Gerrell kept his three sons, Pete, Dale & Lawson, busy building miles of fence for most of that time. Walter Gerrell also hired temporary help from people in Woodville who wanted to work. They fenced through untamed land, cypress ponds and

Remnant of Cypress Base with Notch
Used for climbing the tree to cut it at a higher level.

heavy woodlands. They did not buy fence posts. They cut trees as they went. A lot of cypress and pine were used. To cut the cypress they had to climb part way up the tree and notch foot holds. The base of a cypress was too wide to use. Pines were cut also and then had to be split to fence post size. It was a tough job.

They fenced approximately 1,800 acres of Gerrell family land on the east side of the St Marks River as a start. They then moved across the river and fenced a line west to Wakulla Station. From there the fencing project moved up Woodville Highway and then at the county line it turned back east all the way to the river. At the time, much of this land belonged to the Culbreath family. Mr. Culbreath told them they could fence it to join their land. His condition was he wanted fences on the property lines. This required surveys to know where the lines were. As a result the Culbreaths got some free surveys and the Gerrells were allowed to range their cattle on Culbreath land for many years.

PG

The fence law came in to effect at 12:01 AM July 1, 1949 in Florida. Writing this brought back some unpleasant memories. We had spent two years rounding up cows, building many miles of barbed wire fence, cutting posts and right-of-way for the fence and most of all, watching the old range cows stand by the fence near their old range and die.

The price of our Florida scrub cows, because of the oversupply on the market, had dropped to less than five dollars per hundred pounds. That meant the average cow wouldn't bring $15. They were not worth driving and hauling to the stockyard to sell.

When we started rounding up cows in the spring to mark and brand the calves and sell the steers, we would always go back to these old home sites, use the dogs to trail up the cows or follow the tracks ourselves until we found the herd and could drive them in. We had cow pens in several different places scattered throughout a twenty five mile north to south and twelve mile east to west area which our cows ranged on.

Pete Gerrell was involved with all this as a teenager. It was hard work but a part of him loved it. There were some old turpentine camps in the woods that he would go by to get water and graze on fruit trees such as; plum trees, pear trees, or grapevines as well as other fruits. He stated, "My daddy always accused me of grazing wherever I went. I would go by to get a fruit or a fresh drink of water or just to visit with the old hands".

If we didn't have a permanent pen, there were pens that were made of panels. They were board fences that were built in sections. We could take them to a place, set them up and tie the panels together with wire. We just set up a pen wherever we needed one.

We'd get the calves in during the spring to mark and brand them. The cows that were close to home would be brought to the pen near the house. We'd turn the cows out during the day and keep the calves penned up. The cows would go off to graze in the woods during the day and get their food. Then they would come back at night to nurse the calves. They'd spend the night in the pen with the calves. We'd always take wood and build a smoke or several smokes in the cow pen to keep the flies off the cows. Usually the pen was in a new ground area where we had cut the trees so there were stumps to be burned out. We'd keep the calves shut up until they got big enough to mark and brand. We'd mark and brand them and then turn them out so they could go back to their home range. After we turned the cows out they would go straight back to where we had gotten them from.

Home Cow Pen

Cows in the St. Marks River Circa 1920

I remember one time we were getting up a load of cows to take to the sale on Sunday afternoon. We left the cows in the pen that we didn't want to take to the sale and went ahead and loaded the truck so it would be ready to go on Monday morning. The old fellow that helped with the cows in the woods occasionally also like to drink the strong drink, some of Uncle Rainey's shine or Mr. Johnny's shine. He got to drinking that and he went off and left the cows shut up in the pen. After we left he was going to turn them out.

It was two weeks before we got back. Well the cow pen was a fairly large pen that covered about 150 feet wide and 300 to 400 feet long, so they had a pretty good area there, and it was under big live oak trees. It had some cabbage palmettos in it as well as the moss off the live oak trees and some sprigs of grass, When we finally got back two weekends later, the old cows had eaten up all the moss on the ground and eaten the cabbage palmettos off and had everything cleaned totally up in the pen. They were just about down to the point where they couldn't hardly go.

We never did let Granddaddy know about that because he would have been some kind of upset about his cows not being able to go to the river and feed. This was the river cows that were shut up. We had one herd that probably was 80 to 100 cows that fed in the river basin. They would feed on the river grass. It was a year round green pasture. My brother Dale, and nephew Jim, still have some cows that feed in the river at this time. The river is shallow enough that the cows can walk about halfway across it and get the grass out. We called this herd of cows the basin cows. All we had to do was go down during the day when the cows were in the river feeding. We could go down and holler two or three times and the cows would come out and go to the pen. That was the easiest bunch of cows we had to pen up in the whole herd of about 600 or 800 head of them that we had.

I told you about the cows feeding in the basin during the day. They also fed there at night as well as other animals. The animals have a feeding habit, especially the wild ones, of feeding four times a day. They feed on the different moons. The moon rise is a minor feed time and they feed about a half hour before and a half hour after, for an hour long food time. At south moon over, or when it is directly over, they feed an hour before and an hour after, or a two hour food time. Then at moon set again, it is a minor feed time. At south moon under, which is directly below, the animals feed on a major feed time again, which are an hour before and an hour after. We always could tell when the animals were going to feed.

When the no fence law came into effect, we penned the cows up and put them in a pasture. The price dropped down to about 7 cents a pound for range cows on the hoof so we didn't want to sell them, or give them away - that's what it would have amounted to. It wasn't even worth hauling them to the market. We had probably 100-150 head of cows that tried to get back to their home range. They would go to the fence nearest to their range and stand there beside the fence and die. I've seen places where there were so many dead carcasses and so many bones stacked up that it killed the grass along the fence for 200 yards where cows died.

After we turned the cows out to let them go back to their range with their newly marked and branded calves, we would take that new ground that they had been spending the night on, an area about 200 feet square and we'd plant sweet potatoes on it. We could grow a real good sweet potato crop in that newly fertilized ground. Then the next year we would plant it in sugar cane and it would grow some of the best sugar cane in the country.

Anyway back to 12:01 AM July 1, 1949. Shortly after the law came into effect, one of our herd got through the barbed wire fence and onto a nearby highway. It was a Black Angus bull owned by our grandmother. A gasoline truck hit the bull, killed it and left it lying in the road.

Right after that Robert Rozar and Beverly Pomeroy came along on a motorcycle. There light did not see the dead bull until it was too late and they hit it and went airborne. They were both badly injured but survived to enter suit against us. This caused us to become the first in Florida to be sued because of having unfenced livestock.

One of our friends who lived nearby was trying to be helpful. He cut off the ears of the dead yearling. They were marked with a swallow fork, over and under bit in the right ear and a swallow fork on the left. However, he left the double G (GG) outfit's brand on the right hip. It didn't take long for a deputy to locate the owner of the brand since it had been registered in the county since 1852.

MONTICELLO STOCK YARDS

J. N. HAWKINS, Phone 8-R
W. C. HAWKINS, Phone 8F20

OFFICE Phone 145

P. O. Box 265   MONTICELLO, FLA., _____ 19_5_4_

SOLD FOR _____

ADDRESS _____

We do not guarantee stock against sickness or death. Our responsibility ceases when stock leaves yards. The purchases of live stock listed below agrees that the title of said live stock shall be retained by the Monticello Stock Yards until check or draft is paid. We act as agents only.

Pen No.	No. Head	Descriptions	Markings	Comm.	Weight	Price		Amount	
1				50	195	5	00	9	75
2	1			75	310	5	90	18	29
3	1			50	240	5	00	12	00
4	1			75	310	5	30	16	43
5	1			75	265	6	00	15	90
6	1			50	170	6	00	10	20
7				375					
8	6								
9									
10									
11									
12									
13									
14									
15									
16									
17									
18									
19								82	57
20									

Commission		3 75
		78 82
Yardage		39
Hauling		
Purchases		
Check		78 43

Receipt from 1954 showing low value of beef cattle

We came through that case still owning our land and several hundred head of cattle. The cows would get out but, some of the livestock owners around us would pen them up, notify us, and we would go bring them back to the pasture. By the early 1950s the price had recovered enough that we began selling again. We were then able to reduce the herd to a manageable size within our fenced lands.

CHAPTER NINE

PORK AND HOGS PG

Talking about all these pork recipes reminds me of the fact that we had several hundred head of hogs in the woods and on the open range. They ranged mostly up and down the St. Marks River and in the ponds out from the river. We would raise a crop and, after gathering the crop, would put the hogs in on the remaining fodder. The only way we could get the hogs in was to take catch dogs, catch the hogs and haul them to the fields, to put them in to fatten. My brothers and I would take the catch dogs and horses and go find the hogs. When the dogs caught a hog, we would tie him down and drag him out to the road. Then Daddy would come along, either in the mule and wagon or in later years in an old Jeep with a trailer behind it. We would load the hogs in the trailer and haul them to the house and put them in a pen. We would keep them shut up in a pen for a few days before we turned them into the field. After they got fat, we would bring them in and butcher them.

Hog killing time was a big time. We'd kill fifteen or twenty hogs, usually on a cold November morning starting before daylight. We'd bring the hogs in, kill them and scald them, scraping the hair off. We would cut them up and do all the other things necessary to get a hog ready to eat - to smoke, salt down, make sausage or for whatever we were going to do with it.

One of the nastiest jobs was to strip the **chitlins**; no part of the hog was wasted. I can remember one time when I was too small to help with the hogs. They had been stripping chitlins in a hole out in the back of the old syrup house. If you can just picture what came out of the chitlins, this hole was full of it. We were running and playing hide and seek and I fell into the hole. Needless to say, I had to make a trip to the pond to get cleaned up. I always did like to strip chitlins in the river, though, that was the easy way to do it. I just got out of the boat and stripped them and washed them right into the river

That way all the leavings would go off down the river. I just sort of would pity those folks that were downstream from us.

Salting Meat

Mollie Hall French on Left; Ina French on right

One day we were getting ready to go hog hunting. My brother and I had already saddled our horse when Daddy decided he needed to take the old Jeep and go to the town about three miles away to get some gas. While he was gone, my brother and I were in a ditch out in front of the house and found a pint of whiskey. We took one of the old hog dogs; in fact the best of the hog dogs, and gave him a good big drink of whiskey so he'd really be ready to catch that day. After we gave him the drink of whiskey we just turned him loose. A little while later Daddy came back.

We started off to the woods, got down close to the river, caught a couple of hogs, tied them, drug them out to the road and loaded them into the trailer. The old dog got to feeling his drink and staggering around. Finally he got to the point where he couldn't go and we loaded him into the back of the Jeep. He lay there all afternoon until we got back to the house. That night I was laying in bed listening to Mamma and Daddy talking and I heard Daddy telling Mamma that he guessed he was going to have to kill old Jake. He was going to do away with him, because he acted like he was "down in the back" or had the blind staggers or something. Luckily old Jake was straightened out the next morning. We never told Daddy about doing that to the dog until we were grown and away from home. If we'd have told him about it he would have probably run us off from home.

Cast Iron Sausage Stuffer; Freshly Smoked Sausage

The homemade sausage was also made during the hog killing time. We would trim the lean meat off the backbone and the shoulders and grind it up in an old hand cranked sausage grinder. Then we'd mix ground sage, red pepper, black pepper, salt and maybe some other seasonings with the meat. This would be stuffed into casings, (which was chitterlings) with a hand cranked sausage stuffer.

The sausage was then hung in the smokehouse where it was smoked with the other meat. The smokehouse was an important place at every country home. It is where the meat was cured and kept. We had one behind our house. During the hog killing the pork was cut into pieces, ham, shoulder, thighs and so forth. These pieces were salted down and spread out on the smokehouse floor on green pine straw. The floor of the smokehouse was the ground.

The meat was left this way a couple of weeks. Then it was taken up and the salt was knocked off of it. It was then re-salted and stacked in small piles, again on the clean green pine straw. The piles were covered with salt and green pine straw. After about four weeks, the meat was taken out and the salt knocked off again. Then the meat was hung on the open ceiling joist in the smokehouse on nails. We liked to use bear grass, a tough green blade of grass that we got from the woods to help hang our meat with. The bear grass was tied in a loop through a hole in the meat, then hung over a nail on the smokehouse ceiling joist. The smoke was then built in a hole in the ground in the middle of the smokehouse. We used hickory wood to smoke our meat. The slow smoke was maintained for a week or so, until the meat was cured.

The meat and the sausage were left hanging in the smokehouse with pieces being cut from it as needed. I sure was glad when I got big enough to reach a butcher knife, which was stuck in a post inside the smokehouse door. I'd take the butcher knife and trim a piece of lean, dried meat off and it was better than any chewing gum I'd ever chewed.

Speaking of chewing gum reminds me of the fact that I've never had a toothache or had any problem with my teeth. They've been with me now probably about 55 years. What I credit this to is the fact that during the time my teeth were forming in the years when I was coming up until I was about 20 years old, I was riding in the piney woods where the old turpentine catfaces were. The resin would ball up on the old cat faces. I would ride by and pull a ball of this turpentine off and put it in my mouth and chew it. It crumbled up usually when you first started chewing it, but if you chewed it for three or four minutes it would start to adhere together and after about five minutes of chewing it would be just like chewing gum. I credit my good teeth to the fact that I constantly chewed that rosin. No telling what it did to my insides, but I feel that it did my forming teeth a lot of good.

Bear grass growing on Gerrell Property

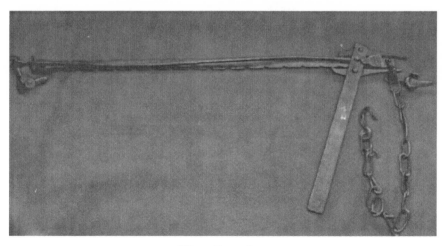

Wire Stretcher
Used to build barb wire fence for hogs & cattle

CHAPTER TEN

HUNTING & FISHING STORIES

HUNTING   <u>PG</u>

I've told you about drinking cane buck on our trip to the camp. That camp was located, as I said, about twelve miles back in the woods from the nearest civilization. It was actually down on what we call the western sloughs. The camp was an old log building that just had a little lean-to kitchen built onto the side of it with an old wood stove in it. The log building was used for sleeping quarters. We would go down there and spend two or three weeks every winter, hunting in the western sloughs. Some of the best hunting in this part of the country was there in that area.

One year before I went to the camp I was bird hunting and a fellow shot me in the arm, just above the wrist. I got an infection from the shot after I got to the camp twelve miles from nowhere. This old man (Identified as Fletcher Tharpe) that had asthma real bad and stayed at the camp with us smoked a pipe with something in it. I really don't know what it was, could have been marijuana. It really smelled good and made you feel good when you were in that closed up building with him smoking at night to clear up his asthma.

My arm got infected and red streaks started running up it and I knew I was in real trouble. He took an old handkerchief and a jar of Vick's salve. He took that jar of Vick's salve and rubbed it on the place and tied the old handkerchief around my arm. Then he made me lay down by the side of the wall and tied my arm up so that I couldn't get it down so it would be higher than the rest of my body. He made me stay there all night with my arm tied up to the side of the wall with a rope.

The next morning I got up and the red streaks had receded back to the place where the shot was. I don't know whether it was lead poisoning, blood poisoning or what. I guess the old man saved my hand and arm that way because I would have been another day or day and a half getting out of those woods.

When we got to the camp one year there was a coon in the well. We used an open well and it was only about 12 or 14 feet deep. There was a coon that had fallen in the well and died. We quite often had to get snakes out of it, but we had it curbed up about two feet so the snakes were not too bad about getting in it. The coon was dead in the well so we got down in the well and got him out with the well bucket and then had to totally bail the water out of the well to let fresh water come back in. We did boil our drinking water for a couple of days until the water cleared up.

We always carried an old Black fellow with us to cook at the camp. One rainy evening we decided we would scare him. He was scared of the bears. They were plentiful then and you could hear them at night falling out of the palm trees. They would get up in the top of a palm tree and mash the top down and pull the bud out. When they pulled the bud out, using their front feet and their teeth, they would simply roll out of the tree and hit the ground. You could hear them hit the ground over a quarter of a mile on a still night. Also, you could hear them climbing the fence.

We were right beside the pasture fence and you could hear the bear climbing it. The old Black cook was real afraid of them. He would stay inside most of the time, but he had to go outside to do most of his cooking on an open fire. He also cleaned what little vegetables we had and he cleaned the smaller game for us, the turkeys, squirrels, and things of that type that we killed and used for food.

On one rainy night, one of the boys took an old black slicker and put it on and the old Black fellow was standing by the fire getting something cooked just about dark. This boy came slipping out of the woods with this black slicker over him and him down crawling, looking like a bear. The old Black fellow went into the kitchen and wouldn't come out. We ended up having to do the outside work because the old Black fellow wouldn't come out. He did the rest of his cooking and cleaning in the house and we ended up having to do what he had been doing outside.

Talking about the bears, I shot an old Sears and Roebuck bolt action shotgun that I had paid $28 for. It held seven shells and was a .12 gauge with a 32" barrel. It would hold a pretty tight pattern over a 50 or 75 yard shot. We jumped a bear and he was running down through the woods.

I heard him coming. He got to a pasture fence and climbed up on top of it. When he got to the top of it, I shot him. He looked at me and climbed down off the fence, turned and looked at me, then started licking the trickle of blood that was running down his side. I was only about 30 steps from him so I decided I had better shoot him again and see if I couldn't kill him and put him out of his misery. On the second shot I was quite excited, I'm sure, but he just turned and looked at me and started running. When he hit one of the sloughs about a quarter of a mile down from where I shot him, one of the boys was there. He heard him hit the slough and said that he separated the waters. It was almost like Moses separating the water in the Red Sea. It took time for it to come back together.

I've told you some things about my Uncle Jim. He was my Daddy's older brother. We simply called him Uncle Natural, that name fit him so well. The strange thing about Uncle Natural was after Uncle Jim died, my nephews and nieces gave me the name of Uncle Natural and some people simply call me Old Natural. I guess I acquired that name. I didn't ever connect myself as being that much like Uncle Jim, but I must be pretty natural in my ways.

Anyway, Uncle Jim Gerrell came down one day. He was a game warden at the time and he had located several coveys of quail. Daddy had two pointer dogs. He and Daddy got together and always had to have a few drinks when they were together. They took their strong drink and put it in a saddle bag and threw the saddles on the old horses.

Uncle Jim used Old Slogan, I'll tell you about him later. They went down quail hunting on the horses. This was after about 1:00. About 3:00, Old Slogan came back to the house with blood draining down his face and it looked like he was bleeding from the head. I went out and caught him. I didn't know where Uncle Natural was. I took the saddle off him and put him in the lot. I looked at his face and he had shotgun shots through his ears.

He had evidently not enjoyed the quail hunting with Uncle Natural and had thrown him off and come back to the house after Uncle Natural put some shot through his ears. A little while later, probably an hour, Daddy and Uncle Natural came riding back to the house on Daddy's horse, Old Preacher. Of course, Old Preacher was a roping horse and he didn't cotton to quail hunting too much either. Daddy was a much better rider than Uncle Jim was because he stayed in the woods all the time with the cows and rode the horses. Anyway, Old Slogan got over it and I'll tell you some more stories about him as time goes by. You'll see where Slogan was known as Slogan the Wonder Horse.

We did a lot of our deer hunting at night with a headlight, usually just a fairly dim light. If it was a bright light we would take a packet handkerchief to dim it down so it wouldn't be so bright. All you wanted to do was see the animal's eyes and the dimmer the light was the closer you could get to the animal whose eyes were shining.

One night we went into the sloughs. We had two blazed trails into the hammock and we took one trail and went on it, just the two of us, another boy (Identified as Bill Tharpe) and me. Two others, the older men, took the other trail and went on it. We separated just before dark. The moon was rising along about 9:00 so we didn't have much time to hunt before the moon got up. You couldn't hunt with the moon full because the animals would see you and spook.

We started early, as soon as it got dark enough that we wouldn't spook the animals. Before we had walked a hundred yards, an old owl hooted. I said, "Boy this sounds good. When the old owl hoots, the animals are feeding." A minor feed time is an hour before and an hour after moon rise and moon set. A major feed time is south moon over and south moon under. That's when the moon is directly overhead and directly under. They feed longer then and there are more of them that feed at that time. Minor feed time, the old owl hooted and we started off.

Bill took the shotgun and light first and was walking. It wasn't hardly any time before he saw one and probably about where the owl hooted. He slipped off while I stayed on the trail. We didn't get off the blazed trail. If you did you were subject to get lost and not find your way out of there for three days.

He killed a deer, a small buck. We field dressed it, cut the legs off it, tied up the skin from the legs so he could strap it and put it on his back. Bill tied his on his back and then I took the light and gun. It wasn't but just a few minutes before I saw one. I killed it. It was a big old doe. We did the same thing with it, strapped it up and we got back to the fork of the trail. The old doe's head was slapping against my leg and I decided to cut it off and carry the deer without the head.

He had the wise thought that we would take that old doe's head and put it on a stump there at the fork of the trail, facing the trail where the other men had gone into the hammock. We did. We went on to the camp, which was about a quarter of a mile. We were about whipped by the time we got there. About the time we got to the camp, the shooting started. These people coming on the other trail had seen the old doe's head sitting on the stump and they shot about 12 times before they finally knocked it off the stump. When they got to the camp they were mighty upset.

These were some of the older men in the camp. We didn't have many shells then anyway. It was right after the Second World War and shells were real scarce. So it ended up we had to walk to the next camp, which was about four miles away and beg them for some shells to replace the ones that these men had shot up the night before at the old doe's head.

One of the most scary things that could happen to you while you were fire hunting with your dim light at night was to walk into a covey of quail. A covey of quail will roost in a circle with their tails all together and when they fly up from being spooked, they will all fly in opposite directions. This covey of quail will make you wish you were somewhere other than in the woods.

One night I was hunting with Bill, the same fellow that was hunting with me when he put the doe's head on the stump. We had given up on finding anything and were headed back to camp. We decided to take a shortcut across this palmetto flat. We were about halfway across the palmetto flat and I was leading with what little bit of light we had left. I stepped on something that was kind of soft and mushy and I didn't know what it was. All of a sudden it came out from under me and it was an old sow and a bunch of pigs. She went off saying, "woof, woof, woof" and I didn't know whether I had another bear cornered or what. By the time I got through walking on the top of those palmettos and getting out to the road that went through the turpentine woods, Bill was just gone. I shot up in the air when the hog ran out from under me. I didn't know whether he had climbed a tree or I had shot him or what, but I hollered for him and he never would come out. I went on back to the camp, which was about three quarters of a mile away. When I got back to the camp he was sitting there at camp waiting for me. He was a little bit scareder than I was.

The Fish and Game Commission likes to take credit for the population of the deer and bear now in comparison to what it was back in the '30s and '40s. I don't think it's the credit of the Fish and Game Commission, but the credit of the Department of Agriculture that the game has increased like it has. Naturally, the Fish and Game Commission and their regulations have done a lot for it, but there was what they called a "screw fly".

When you marked and branded calves we had to hold them up to make sure that this screw fly didn't lay eggs on the open cut. The eggs hatch and the screw worms hatch out and live in the open cuts. This was probably what caused a lot of the decline of the population in wildlife. In the years before the screw fly was eradicated by the Department of Agriculture, there were many cases of the deer and bear and other wild animals getting scratches or cut places on them, especially buck deer from fighting. Anytime a scratch got on an animal, the screw fly would lay its eggs and then this maggot-like worm would hatch and it would continue to eat until it killed the animal. The Department of Agriculture eradicated the screw fly in the early 1950s by sterilizing the male flies. They are no more and the game has really flourished since that time.

I told you about the boy that rode the mule. He wasn't quite right, a little bit off in the head. His Daddy, Carl Maples was probably about the same mentality. He really thought he was a big shot. I don't know what he thought his qualifications were or where he got all of his experience to be qualified for such a thing, but he ran for Governor of the State of Florida twice. Both times he got beat out pretty bad. Fact is, I don't know that he got but one vote the first time, because his wife didn't vote for him. The second time I think his son was old enough to vote so, his son voted for him and he got two votes. Anyway, he ran for Governor.

One night he and Daddy had been out and I always went along for the ride or to drive home. Daddy was driving a new 1941 Ford and he carried the old fellow to his house. It was dark. He pulled up in a lane between two fences and I was in the back seat asleep. He let the old man out and when he started to turn around to go back out the lane, he backed up on top of an old cow. That woke me up. When that old cow started trying to come out from under the car she couldn't make it. We couldn't drive forward off of her either. We ended up waiting until daylight and jacked up the car so we could drag the old cow out from under it. She actually kicked and reared until she tore about half of her hide off one side. The muffler had burned her pretty bad. She was in pretty pitiful condition. Needless to say we didn't get any sleep that night. We did get the car off the top of the cow and the car wasn't much worse for the wear. I think the cow tore loose some brake fluid lines, and some taillight wires, but that was about all the damage the car suffered.

Anyway, the old man Maples thought he was a big shot. He always owned a big gun of some kind, an expensive gun. Usually somebody had given it to him. I don't know whether it was a campaign promise or how he got the gun. He had bought this farm, though; I don't really know what he had to buy it with. His wife was a school teacher, so possibly she was making enough money to support the old man and buy the farm, too. I never knew him to work or do anything other than talk big and run his mouth.

Talking about cooking fish, some of the best fish I ever ate was cooked on an open fire. It was seasoned with salt and pepper, put on a stick and stuck out over the fire to cook. I learned this trick from an old man we called Mr. Johnny that I used to go cat fishing with down on the Creeks between Natural Bridge and the rise of the river. (Mr. Johnny was a local by the name of Johnny Miller.) Mr. Johnny would set out bush hooks – that's a hook and line tied off to the bushes.

We used a nut or a washer to weight the lines down with. Then we baited the hooks with bird or squirrel guts or whatever we happened to have that we could put on the hooks to attract a catfish. The more smelly it was the better it was. We'd set those bush hooks out along about dark or a few minutes before, then about 10:00 we'd "work the bush hooks" (go back and check them) There was usually about twenty or twenty five hooks. We would get the catfish off and rebait the hooks. When we got to the place we were camping, which was just a wide open campfire and camp site, we would skin the catfish and filet them. Then we took the filet of catfish, seasoned it, put it on a stick and cooked it in that way, mainly because we didn't have any other way to cook it. That sure did taste good. Course by that time of the night, we were real hungry and anything would have tasted good.

Another thing that comes to mind about the fish is that we would set traps (fish baskets) in the creeks. The fish swimming upstream to feed would swim into the funnel-like mouth of the basket and couldn't get out. We would place traps in the mouth of about a half dozen creeks and work them the next day. One day, after working the traps, we came back up the river, chugging along with an old 5 horsepower Firestone outboard motor which was about wore out (this all was going on during the second World War). When we got back to the boat landing the game warden was standing on the bank waiting for us so we just kept chugging along up the river and went on up to the basin landing, about a half a mile upstream. We put our bucket of fish out on the hill, come back down the river and got out at the landing.

The game warden asked us what we'd been doing and we just told him we'd been checking the cows. At that time we had about 80 or 100 head of cattle that fed in the river on the river grass, so there wasn't anything unusual about us riding the river and checking on that herd of cows. Se we just let the game warden go on, then went by the basin landing and picked up our bucket of fish.

Another thing we did to get fish was went gigging. We would take this same old cypress flat bottom boat; put a rig on the front of it that went out and up about six feet high. It had a wagon wheel like affair that hung under, this boom that went out. We would build a fire on that wagon wheel like rig out of old fat lighter wood, which is the heart of dead pine trees. Back then we'd get the best of the fat lighter wood to use for what we'd call "giggin wood". We'd cut it up into small pieces, which we'd use to make light to gig by.

We had a five prong gig on a 14 foot handle and we'd get out there in the river, which was shallow in the basin area. The basin area is about a mile long and a quarter of a mile wide. We'd get out there in the river and kill the fish with the gig and put them in the boat. I was pushing along (poling the boat) while Daddy was gigging. He said something about killing gars, that the Game and Freshwater Fish Commission had put a fifty cent bounty on gars' tails. For every tail we turned in we'd get fifty cents. Later I asked him why they were paying that bounty and he said because the gars were killing so many fish.

Well, that night about midnight we started into the basin landing and I got to thinking about it. We had several different species of bream, bass and catfish and we even had some mullet. I said, "Daddy, what kind of bounty do you think the Game Commission would put on our tails if they caught us with all these fish?" He just laughed and said, "Boy, don't worry about that, we gotta eat."

Next thing we had to do was clean the fish. We would just take the fish, filet him, cut his head off, take his guts out and spread him in a barrel. Then we'd take salt and put a layer of fish and a layer of salt in the barrel to preserve them for later use. We would take out what we wanted to eat for breakfast (We always ate them for breakfast.) We'd put them in a pan of fresh water and soak them overnight to get as much of the salt out as we could, then the next morning we'd meal them and fry them in hog lard. We'd take the meal that had toasted and rose to the top of the grease and put it over some grits. Momma always had some biscuits fixed, so that was the way we started our day on the days we had salt fish.

To get you more familiar with this river I'm talking about – it rose and made into a big basin area, which is where we would do our fish gigging. This basin has clear water because it is spring fed. It is about a mile up and down and a quarter of a mile wide. We didn't have any problem with other people bothering us because Granddaddy owned the land from almost a mile north of the rise down to two and a half miles south of the basin. He also owned the land on both sides of the river, so we were pretty well isolated. There were two sets of rapids down river that only the smallest of boats could come across. You would have to be running a pretty good motor and know how to get through the rapids to be able to get up the river to us. So we were pretty well protected and on our own.

CHAPTER ELEVEN

HORSES I KNEW <u>PG</u>

I'm going to reach way back in my memory and start talking about some horses that I've known in my lifetime. The first one was a Shetland pony that my Daddy bought for me and brought home. He was about the smallest thing I'd ever seen in the way of a horse. Daddy bought the saddle to go with him, a little saddle, and a little bridal.

Pete Gerrell 1933
Already learning to ride

I was already big enough that I had ridden horses many times and knew well how to ride horses. I'd never owned one of my own. This one was mine. Finally, I had gotten my own horse. I looked at him and he looked at me and I guess we realized we were going to be together for a while. I saddled him up and that Shetland pony lasted probably about six months under me. I have a habit of being real bad or hard on horses and he didn't last long under me before I outgrew him and my feet were dragging the ground and we had to get another one.

Another thing, he couldn't stand up in the woods with the rough woods and the cows that we had and the work we had to do with him. He just wasn't man enough to take that. Anyway, he lasted about six months and I don't remember him doing anything fantastic or outlandish, except possibly falling down with me two or three times after he stepped in a gopher hole.

From there, I got a horse that was blind in one eye. At the same time, my younger brother got his first horse, which was a mare named Sarah. I'll tell you about Sarah first, because she was a real doozy. That was some kind of a horse. She was what was known as a "stump sucker." She would get a hold of the top board of the horse lot or fence or wherever she was. The fences were built out of either split rails or fat pine boards. She would get a hold of the top board with her top teeth and bite down over the board and pull her top teeth back on the board. She would pull back just as hard she could. It was so hard that she would tear the board off the fence or whatever the board was fastened to. That's why they called her a stump sucker. Originally the horse had some kind of disease. The horses had nothing to pull their top jaw on but a stump, so they would hang their teeth over a stump and backup and pull. Anyway, that horse was a stump sucker.

The only dealings I ever had with her, and I don't know why I was riding her instead of my brother riding her, but I was. We were driving a herd of cows, probably 40 head, through the open piney woods. One of the cows broke and left the herd and old Sarah and I went after the cow. We come on this place that this cow went around and I was going through it, Sarah and I, more Sarah than me because, it was just turn the horse loose and let her go. We were going through this place and it looked just like a puddle of water to me. It was probably 30 feet across but it didn't look like a hole that had any depth to it. I just let her go and she ran into it. There wasn't anything left floating but my hat. One of the boys that was riding with us hollered at me when he saw what was going on and told me to get on the horse's neck so the horse couldn't get on top of me. I wasn't worried about getting on the horse's neck; I was worried more about getting out of that water hole. So I just swam and got my hat and by the time Sarah tried to get to me to get on top of me I'd already hit the hill and was waiting for her to come out on the hill. I got back in the saddle, went around the water hole, kept going and finally caught the yearling and took it back to the herd. That was about the only thing old Sarah ever did to me. I'm sure that my brother had many occasions he could tell you about with her.

The other horse that Daddy got for me at the same time he got Sarah for my brother was just an old nag. When I say nag, it was about that. It didn't have but one eye. The man that sold it to us didn't bother to tell us that it had a glass eye. The pine trees were fairly close together and a lot of our cows ranged in areas where there were crab apple trees and other kinds of trees that were close together.

This one eyed horse couldn't tell whether there was something on his one side or not. He would run between two trees and almost scrape me off. I found myself many times laying down on top of the horse and putting my feet right straight out the back to keep from being drug off by the trees. Needless to say, that horse didn't last too long either. I don't think he even lasted long enough to name him. If he did, I don't remember what his name was.

After the saddle that was on the Shetland pony, I never had another saddle in my life that was any good. They were always hand me down things that came down from some of the uncles or one of the grandfathers or somebody else in the family. The saddles were not the best; they had already been worn out by the time they got handed down to me. They may have had stirrups or they may not have. One of the girths may be missing. There were no saddle bags at all. I'd borrow saddle bags when I was going to stay overnight. I'd get saddle bags from somebody else and tie them on my saddle.

The old saddles were no good at all. There wasn't any use in trying to rope a cow off of it. I'd tie the cows off to the saddle horn several times and that's the way I ended up getting me another worn out saddle. I tied the rope off to the saddle horn and when the cow hit the end of the rope the saddle came apart and just ripped the whole thing out from under the front of me. So I ended up inheriting another used saddle from somebody.

This was also bad for the old horses that I rode. The saddles were worn out and the saddles would rub sores on their backs. The poor old

16horse most of the time had a sore worn on his back in one place or another. The blankets under the saddles were about the same as the saddles. They had all been worn out. The manner of horse that I rode didn't really deserve much more than that.

By the way I rode the horse, maybe, I didn't really deserve much more than that. Because of my back hurting me so bad from time to time, I would ride on the saddle sideways, or sitting with one leg over the saddle, the calf of my leg supporting me on it, if you can picture that. My rear end was not in the saddle, it was sitting off to the side. I would sit behind the saddle and sometimes I'd just take the saddle off and ride totally without it. I rode in all manners of ways. Needless to say, the old horses didn't fare so well under me because of it. Anyway, this one eyed horse would carry me through some of the worst places and I'd end up having to lie down on his back to get through them. He didn't last long either.

Pete Gerrell c. mid 1940s

Along about that time my Granddaddy, Jim French, gave me a horse that was named Blue Pete. It was a blue roan horse and he was not like the hand me down saddles, even though he was a hand me down horse. He was extremely good and very gentle and was able to stand up under me pretty well. I guess I got closer to and treated Blue Pete with more respect than any other horse I'd ever owned.

Blue Pete had worked with the cows enough that he knew about what to do when a cow broke the bunch and started to run into a pond or something. He knew to go ahead and cut it off and get it back into the herd so we could continue to drive it. It was almost like just sitting there and letting Blue Pete do his thing. The only place I ever had any problems with him was riding with the old man over to the east of us that had 1200 or 1500 head of cows.

His name was Lige Granthum.   I'd ride with him occasionally and he always rode big Tennessee walking horses. His horse would be riding along with a gate that you could almost sit in the saddle and go to sleep on. When his was walking that way, mine had to jog to keep up with him, so I was riding along on my horse at a back breaking jog when the other fellow was just sitting up there dozing in the saddle. I don't remember how many years Blue Pete was with me but, probably for about four years altogether. I had ridden him before Granddaddy had given him to me, so it's hard to know just when he became mine, when I started to take care of him as mine and keep him at the house where I lived instead of at Granddaddy's house. That was my Granddaddy French over on the river.

I started to keep Blue Pete at our house. One Saturday, I had saddled up Blue Pete and got the dogs. We always did that every weekend, Saturday and Sunday. We had to get up cows or hogs to take to the market on Monday. We had usually at least one load of cows or hogs at the sale. That particular Monday we were going to have a load of hogs and we lacked a few of having enough, so I took Blue Pete and saddled him up. Then I took the dogs and went down into what we called "Clara Bay," which was about four miles southeast of the house, down on the St. Marks River.

I spent the afternoon down there catching hogs and tying them down. The dogs would bay them and catch them. I'd go in and get them by the hind leg and pull them down and tie them with the pigging strings. Then I'd take old Blue Pete, tie a rope on them and drag them out to the side of the road. Then Daddy could come along with the mule and wagon and pick them up, put them in it and bring them back to the house.

After we got through catching the hogs I was on the way home and I had a pretty hot afternoon catching hogs. It was getting late and we got to a creek and I got off and got me a drink of water. The dogs drank downstream from me. Blue Pete got him a drink of water. We headed on to the house. Before we got home, about two miles, Blue Pete was so sick that he couldn't carry me any further and I had to get off and walk and lead him. By the time I got to the house I was beginning to get sick myself.

I was actually sick for several weeks after that. It must have been something in the water, although it didn't affect the dogs. I was sick for several weeks after that and spent several days in the hospital in an isolation ward because they didn't know what was wrong with me. When I got out of the hospital and came home, I wasn't told right off, but it wasn't long before I realized that something was missing, my horse. Blue Pete had died during the time I was in the hospital. They finally told me about it afterwards, after I got to missing him and wanting to know where he was. So, I lost Blue Pete in that manner.

That trip to the hospital was quite a stay. I was there actually eight days and it was an old Army hospital where the army had moved out after the war was over. The city took it over and was running it. The room they put me in had a little glass window in the door of it. The nurses would come by and look through the window at me and that was about as close as they would get to me because no one knew what I had. Old Dr. Rhodes was doctoring me and he never did diagnose what it was, mainly because he didn't know.

Anyway, my Maw and Daddy would come to see me and they would stand there and look at me through that glass. Finally, my temperature went down to the point where the doctor said he didn't think I was contagious anymore (if I had been at all to begin with). He let the nurses and my mother and daddy start coming in to see me then. That was after about seven days. It was quite a trip to the hospital that I had there to be a teenage boy and not really understanding what was going on in the world anyway.

After I overed that, Daddy got me another horse. This was the horse of all horses. My sister named him; she named him Slogan, Slogan the Wonder Horse. He was not able to stand up under me hardly at all when I was in the woods riding him. We hardly ever went anywhere without Slogan falling down with me and throwing me out of the saddle or doing something like that. We stayed on the ground more than we stayed up walking.

Anyway, Slogan was the same one that Uncle Jim shot the ears off of. I guess he had a reason to not necessarily want somebody on his back. I'll take you through some of the old trips that Old Slogan and I had. We were driving a herd of 30 or 40 head of cows from a place over to the east of the river and carrying them down to the cow pen at Granddaddy's house on the east side of the St. Marks river. This was probably three miles. One of the steers broke and Slogan and I took off after the steer. There had been an old gas line that came through our land during the Second World War and they came through and dug up the gas line and left these big holes in the woods where the gas line was.

There had also been a telegraph line, or communications line, along this gas line. They had telephones located along it, it was a line that ran from Carrabelle to Jacksonville and was used to pipe the gasoline across the state rather than carrying it around the state. They'd bring it down from Texas into Carrabelle and then across to Jacksonville, where they'd use it. The barges would off load it in Carrabelle and the war ships or whatever in Jacksonville would use it.

Anyway, they'd left these holes open and Slogan and I were going across the woods after the steer that had broke and run. All of a sudden, we hit one of those holes. The girths on the old saddle I had broke and the saddle and me went on across the ditch and hit on the other side of it. I hit the ground still in the saddle, but minus the horse. One of the stirrups came over (yeah, the saddle had stirrups) and hit me just upside of the head and when it did it knocked me out. The next thing I knew was when I woke up.

I looked around and couldn't see my horse anywhere. I got up and staggered around and found my horse lying upside down in the ditch. He couldn't turn over so I tried to roll him over and he couldn't roll over. I heard my brother Dale holler about that time and I climbed out of the ditch and hollered for him to come help me. Well, Old Slogan was laying there with all four feet sticking straight up and him turned upside down in the ditch. We looked the situation over and I told my brother, "well, he can't come out like he is, so take your lariat rope and I'll tie it off around him and will see if we can roll him over and get him out." So that's what we did.

When we rolled him over Old Slogan come out from the ditch just pawing and scraping. He was ready to get up and get out of there. Poor old thing had sweated so bad the hole behind his eye (horses have a cave behind their eyes) was filled with sweat and it was pouring out of it

123

when we finally got him out of that hole. They say that you can judge a horse's age by the depth of that hole behind his eye. They say the deeper the hole is the older the horse is. Old Slogan must have been 75 or 100 years old because that hole would hold probably a half pint of sweat, and that's about how much he had in it.

Anyway, I got Old Slogan out, got him up and put the saddle back on him. I tied it off as best I could. I sent Dale on to catch the cow and get it back in the bunch. I got back on Old Slogan and he and I went on and probably stumbled two or three more times that day before we finally got the cows in the pen. It was a long day for he and I both. Old Slogan could run so hard and fast that it looked like his front legs were rolling over, like wheels with spokes in them, instead of going out. When he started running he had a habit of sticking his head straight out forward, his nose straight out ahead of him and taking the bits in his mouth and he would go where he wanted to. Usually, I ended up having to throw him down in some way to get him stopped. That was always a hard trip when I hit the ground with a horse possibly getting on top of me, and sometimes he did.

My brother, by that time, had gotten him a little pinto horse that was real small. He was fast as a calico cat. He could really go. We were betting on the horses and whose horse could outrun whose. Soon after my brother had gotten his pinto we were going out from the house on a lane that ran about a quarter of a mile, with a fence on each side of the road. Then, there was about another half quarter to the highway, which had just been paved with fresh asphalt. It was in the fall of the year. We decided we'd race the horses down that lane for the quarter of a mile and see which horse could outrun the other.

Well, little Old Slogan pulled one of his tricks and got his nose stuck straight out and his bits in his mouth and in his teeth. I couldn't control him and he was going down the road. There was no way I could get a hold of anything I could pull him down with. He went to the end of that lane and my brother's horse pulled up and stopped. Old Slogan just kept going.

There was an old sharecropper that lived across the highway from us about three quarters of a mile and he just happened to be coming back from delivering a wagon load of vegetables to the fruit market. He was coming back in his mule and wagon and was in the road there when I got to the highway with Slogan running as hard as he could run.

Well, I got him to turn before he got to the wagon and when he hit the pavement his feet slid out from under him and he slid all the way under the wagon. When he did, I got a terrible case of asphalt rash down my left side. When he went under the wagon his teeth hit the metal rim on the back wagon wheel and knocked loose all of his top teeth in the front of his mouth. It just loosened them off where pieces of them were chipped off and falling out. I don't remember just what the old man said when we went under the wagon, but I do know that it was quite a jolt to him as well as to Old Slogan and me. Anyway, I got Old Slogan back up and got him out of the road.

Slogan and I walked back to the house, three quarters of a mile. When we got back, Daddy came out and looked at him. He knew that something was wrong with me coming back walking my horse because I wouldn't walk anywhere. In fact, I didn't hardly know how to walk until I went into the service at eighteen years old. I did learn how to walk then. Anyway, he knew something was wrong so he come out and took one look at the old horse's bleeding mouth and his busted front teeth. Then, again, the strong language came and he used some pretty stiff words at me. He told me that I was going to have to chew the old horse's corn for him from then on until his mouth got well. I sure was glad that horse's mouth was well pretty soon. Of course, Old Slogan loved to eat anyway and he wouldn't have allowed me to chew his food for him for very long.

I told you about the crab apple trees. We had a herd of cattle that were down at St. Marks. They ranged along the St. Marks and Wakulla Rivers and usually around the old fort. This was before it was restored. We had the cows there. We had cow pens scattered over the countryside. The nearest cow pen to there was about halfway to Wakulla Station, above where Highway 98 crosses the St. Marks Highway now. Anyway, we gathered those cows up from down there and started them up to the pen there, which was just off the road. We just decided that what we would do is take the cows right up the highway and that's what we did. They have paved the highway to St. Marks because they'd run gas trucks down there, but there wasn't hardly any traffic on it in those days except for gas trucks. Many people were not able to own vehicles then. So, we just drove the cows up the highway rather than ride through those crab apple trees. Maybe the local people knew that the crab apple trees had thorns on them and that it was the worst place in the world to ride a horse.

It was on one of those same trips in that area that Daddy's horse got in a fight with another horse and got one of his hind legs broken. Daddy's horse was Old Preacher and I rode Preacher whenever I could, when Daddy wasn't riding him. He was such an easy horse to work in the woods. He knew how to work the woods and he knew how to work the cows. He was a good roping horse and a good cutting horse, too. A good cutting horse means good at separating the cows out inside of the pen.

Old Preacher was bad about when you put the saddle on him. He would take in a real deep breath. After you got the saddle tightened up, he would let out his breath and you had to ride him a little ways and then get off and tighten the saddle again when he wasn't expecting you to do it so that you could have your saddle on tight. Well, I put the saddle on and we went up to the cow pen to cut out some steers to take to the market. Daddy was riding him in the pen and cutting out the steers and the saddle went sideways and come off the horse. When it did, Daddy caught himself and broke his arm and wrist. I felt real bad about that because I had ridden Old Preacher up to the cow pen, which was about a quarter of a mile, and I didn't tighten the saddle back up. Of course, I guess Daddy was as guilty as I was because he knew Preacher's habits.

I won't ever forget that night, after we took Daddy to the doctor and the doctor put a cast on his arm. We went back and were spending the night on the river that night in the old house over there. Daddy's arm swelled up in that cast and we had a couple of uncles there and they had all been drinking pretty heavy, the strong stuff. When Daddy's arm swelled up in the cast and he had gotten some pain medication and some alcohol mixed, he didn't feel any pain until a little later on in the night. Then he woke up during the night and I remember hearing one of my uncles say that he was going to have to go get the ax and take care of Daddy.

I got to wondering what in the world he was going to do to Daddy with the ax. He went and got the saw instead of getting the ax and he kidded Daddy about knocking him in the head with the ax and putting him out of his misery. He sawed that cast off of him and wrapped it up. He left the cast open and sawed off and tied it back up a little looser with a towel and some rags. He went on back to bed after taking a few more drinks and another pain pill and slept the rest of the night away.

Anyway, Old Preacher was a good horse and there was nothing we could do after he got his hind leg broke except to have him put to sleep. We paid another black fellow to take him out and shoot him and bury him. That was about a sad day for all of us because we had been so close to Old Preacher. He had been with us for ten or twelve years and was an extremely good horse.

Back to Old Slogan the Wonder Horse, we were getting a load of cows together on Sunday afternoon to take to a sale on Monday morning. One of the steer yearlings that we wanted to load and take broke the bunch. It got out of the pen and took off down through the field. When it did, I went to get my horse. He was the closest horse, Old Slogan. My brother went to get his pinto.

The dogs took off after the cow seeing that we were going to go after it. I was the lead horse and the dogs caught the cow at about half a quarter mile from the pen. When the dogs caught it, I was close enough to it that it turned and went under my horse, right in front of my horse and the horse went across it.

By the time my brother got there to help me get up and get out of the mess I was in, Old Slogan was laying on top of me and the cow was down in the pile with the dogs. There was the cow and the dogs and the horse, all of them on top of me, and the horse wouldn't get up. My brother got the dogs and the cows straightened out and the old horse wouldn't get up off me. I pulled my pocket knife out and opened it up and stuck him in the shoulder good with it at the same time I was raking my spurs across him with the leg that I did have free. Anyway, Old Slogan decided it was time to get up when I started sticking at him with a pocket knife. That was a real tangled up mess that we were in.

I don't rightfully remember what ever happened to Old Slogan. Just one of those things that came to pass, I guess. I probably could tell more stories to tell about him. Most of them were falls that we had because he was constantly falling in a gopher hole or a stump hole or something like that. Or either I was having to throw him down to stop him. There was always times when he and I were both on the ground trying to get up. I don't know how either one of us lived through the trips that we took. Like I say, I don't know what ever happened to Slogan. I know I didn't kill him so he probably was still there in the pasture when I went off to the service during the Korean War.

I didn't say it before, but Old Slogan was less than a quarter horse. He was probably only about 1/8th horse. The rest was fool.

One thing for sure, I didn't have to worry about anyone else wanting to take him away from me or ride him. My youngest brother, Lawson, was not able to toe him down when he got his head stuck straight out in front like he did and got his bits up between his teeth so he couldn't control him. So he didn't care about riding him.

My other brother, Dale, had a little pinto called Tony that he was crazy about, so I didn't have to worry about anybody running out to saddle my horse and take off with him. I was the only one that would ride him and I guess the only reason why I would was because I was just flat stuck with him and didn't have any other way to go. Like I say, I didn't walk very far. I reckon the only time I really got off and walked was when Blue Pete got sick and I had to walk him home because he wasn't able to carry me. And then Old Slogan went under the wagon and tore his front teeth out, and he wasn't able to carry me, so I had to get off and walk then. Other than that, I didn't walk very far, didn't really have any need to. So, Slogan and I had some long trips. There were times when we would go all the way from the house down to the lighthouse and I would ride him down there and we'd come back to as far as Granddaddy's house on the river and spend the night over there.

IN CONCLUSION TG

This is 2012, about 185 years after the time Elizabeth Byrd Hall ventured to Florida as a lone widow. She not only managed to carve a home out of the wilderness, but perhaps more important she established a family legacy that continues to affect the North Florida region.

Many of her direct descendents still live here in Leon and Wakulla Counties on or close to the St Marks River. Family still owns the land Elizabeth lived on. What once she and her family worked so hard to clear and tame, we have replanted and turned back into a Florida forest. The land is managed forestland and the family is active in the timber and forestry industry. The photo of a rainbow showing over the pine trees on the cover, was recently taken looking over that forest from the site of the Hall Place Homestead.

The Gerrell branch of the family that bought land a few miles away in the late 1800s also left a legacy. Some of the family members also live on that land. My home and the home of my grandsons sit on land where the tomatoes and sweet potato crops were that Pete Gerrell so hated to water as a child.

Perhaps there is no need to find the diamond brooch after all. This land and the families it has raised can be considered the diamonds and the treasures at the end of the rainbow.

Pete Gerrell and his Grandson Josh c.1999. Planting Pine Trees with a Dibble on Land Adjacent to the Hall Place Home Site

APPENDIX A

FIELD SPECIMEN LIST

FS #	Weight	Length/Dimensions	Description	Material	Comments
1	< 1 g	1.5 cm	button	brass	eagle insignia
2	< 1 g	1.4 cm	button	brass	eagle insignia
3	< 1 g	1.4 cm	button	brass	eagle insignia
4	< 1 g	2.0 cm	button	brass	eagle insignia surrounding "I"
5	< 1 g	2.0 cm	button	brass	eagle insignia surrounding "R"; reverse side marked with "WM Smith · New York"
6	3 g	2.1 cm	button	brass	General Service, eagle insignia
7	< 1 g	2.2 cm	button	brass	convex shape, eagle insignia surrounded by ring of stars
8	< 1 g	2.0 cm	button	brass	eagle insignia surrounding "A"; reverse side marked with "W·H·PHI·Horstmann & Sons"
9	< 1 g	1.5 cm	button	brass	eagle insignia
10	< 1 g	2.0 cm	button	brass	eagle insignia surrounding "D"; reverse side marked with "WM·H Smith Co · New York"
11	< 1 g	1.5 cm	button	brass	eagle insignia
12	< 1 g	1.8 cm	button	brass	eagle insignia surrounding "C"; reverse side marked with "Adolfo Roemsch · Manila"
13	< 1 g	1.4 cm	button	brass	eagle insignia

FS #	Weight	Length/Dimensions	Description	Material	Comments
14	22 g	3.2 cm x 5.5 cm	part of horse bridle	metal	marked with "US"
15	54 g	6.2 cm x 3.5 cm	belt plate	brass	"CS" for Confederate States; reverse side marked with "1862" and "P"
16	14 g	7.2 cm x 2.9 cm	gun swivel	lead	
17	6 g	3.8 cm x 3.4 cm	boot heel	lead	star cutout, and possible tack hole
18	12 g	7.7 cm x 4.5 cm	belt buckle	brass	floral design
19	124 g	12.8 cm x 12.7 cm	stirrup	lead	
20	186 g	8.2 cm x 7.5 cm	handcuff	iron	
21	433 g	55.5 cm x 8.6 cm	handcuff with chain	iron	not known if connected to FS 20
22	28 g	5.3 cm	breastplate	brass	Confederate; dented
23	28 g	5.3 cm	breastplate	brass	Confederate
24	89 g	6.1 cm x 6.9 cm	breastplate	brass	Union; bullet hole
25	8 g	1.0 cm	case shot	lead	
26	10 g	1.1 cm	case shot	lead	
27	12 g	1.2 cm	case shot	lead	
28	26 g	1.4 cm	case shot	lead	
29	26 g	1.7 cm	case shot	lead	
30	26 g	1.4 cm	case shot	lead	
31	24 g	1.4 cm	case shot	lead	
32	32 g	2.5 cm x 1.5 cm x 1.5 cm	Minié Ball	lead	3-ring Minié ball, .69 cal
33	32 g	2.7 cm x 1.5 cm x 1.5 cm	Minié Ball	lead	3-ring Minié ball, .69 cal
34	16 g	2.3 cm	Minié Ball	lead	3-ring Minié ball, .69 cal; deformed
35	103 g	14.0 cm	case shot mold	brass	
36	9 g	2.1 cm x 4.0 cm	padlock cover	metal	broken at tip; eagle insignia marked with "W.W. & Co."
37	<1 g	1.3 cm	unknown	metal	shield-shaped
38	10 g	1.8 cm	unknown	metal	
39	5 g	2.6 cm x 1.2 cm	percussion cap can	tin	
40	15 g	4.0 cm x 1.8 cm	percussion cap can	tin	may contain something - rust?
41	16 g	4.8 cm x 1.9 cm	percussion cap can	tin	may contain something - rust?

FS #	Weight	Length/Dimensions	Description	Material	Comments
42	10 g	5.0 cm	casing	brass	.50 cal casing; end marked with "U.M.C. 50-EX"
43	10 g	4.6 cm	casing	brass	.50 cal casing
44	5 g	2.7 cm	casing	brass	.50 cal casing
45	3 g	2.6 cm	casing	brass	.50 cal casing
46	33 g	2.3 cm x 2.3 cm x 1.0 cm	cannon ball fuse	iron	
47	74 g	4.1 cm x 4.1 cm x 2.9 cm	cannon ball fuse	iron	
48	99 g	3.5 cm x 3.5 cm x 3.1 cm	cannon ball fuse	iron	
49	< 1 g	3.4 cm	cannon fuse striker	metal	
50	8 g	1.1 cm	case shot	lead	
51	6 g	1.3 cm	case shot	lead	lip on edge
52	< 1 g	1.4 cm	case shot (?)	unknown	
53	12 g	1.4 cm	case shot	lead	
54	19 g	1.4 cm	case shot	lead	
55	15 g	1.4 cm	case shot	lead	
56	14 g	1.3 cm	case shot	lead	
57	17 g	1.4 cm	case shot	lead	
58	26 g	1.7 cm	case shot	lead	
59	26 g	1.8 cm	case shot	lead	
60	24 g	1.8 cm	case shot	lead	
61	8 g	1.8 cm	case shot	lead	
62	7 g	1.6 cm	case shot	lead	
63	9 g	2.0 cm	case shot	lead	
64	16 g	2.0 cm	case shot	lead	
65	19g	1.9 cm	case shot	lead	
66	32 g	2.1 cm	grapeshot	lead	
67	40 g	2.7 cm	grapeshot	lead	
68	25 g	2.8 cm	grapeshot	lead	
69	44 g	3.2 cm x 5.5 cm	grapeshot	lead	
70	1717 g	11.5 cm x 11.0 cm	exploding shell fragment	iron	1/2 of a 12-lb. cannon ball; fuse hole visible
71	1015 g	11.2 cm x 10.6 cm	exploding shell fragment	iron	1/2 of a 12-lb. cannon ball

FS #	Weight	Length/Dimensions	Description	Material	Comments
72	1241 g	11.1 cm x 11.0 cm	exploding shell fragment	iron	1/2 of a 12-lb. cannon ball; fuse hole visible
73	100 g	7.0 cm x 3.5 cm	exploding shell fragment	iron	
74	5444 g	11.0 cm x 11.0 cm	exploding shell	iron	whole 12-lb. cannon ball
75	45.4 kg		exploding shell	iron	siege mortar with intact cannon fuse hole
76	881 g	28.5 cm	pistol	metal	.44 cal Tranter Double action revolver
77	372 g	13.5 cm x 15.2 cm	stirrup	lead	
78	103 g	2.9 cm	canister shot	lead	possibly fired
79	153 g	3.2 cm	canister shot	lead	
80	174 g	4.2 cm	canister shot	lead	
81	245 g	3.6 cm	canister shot	lead	
82	287 g	4.0 cm	canister shot	lead	
83	490 g	4.7 cm	canister shot	lead	
84	528 g	5.2 cm	canister shot	lead	
85	177 g	18.0 cm x 6.5 cm	bayonet	Metal	triangular blade; broken
86	367 g	46.7 cm x 7.7 cm	bayonet	Metal	triangular blade
87	571 g	25.7 cm x 2.7 cm	gun barrel	Metal	exploded
88	1905 g	103.0 cm x 3.2 cm	gun barrel	Metal	exploded
89	2052 g	118.1 cm x 2.4 cm	gun barrel	Metal	whole
90 & 91	1074 g	90: 37.8 cm x 2.8 cm; 91: 36.0 cm x 2.5 cm	gun barrel	Metal	two busted pieces rusted together
92	1072 g	51.8 cm x 2.8 cm	gun barrel	Metal	exploded
93	1220 g	63.5 cm x 2.8 cm	gun barrel	metal	exploded
94	429 g	28.2 cm x 1.2 cm	gun barrel	metal	exploded and bent
95	700 g	10.5 cm x 10.5 cm	unknown	metal mix	

(Barnett, 2011)

APPENDIX B <u>TG</u>

The following are some photos of some of the artifacts found by the Gerrell family over the years on family property in and around Natural Bridge.

Variety of Metal Military Buttons

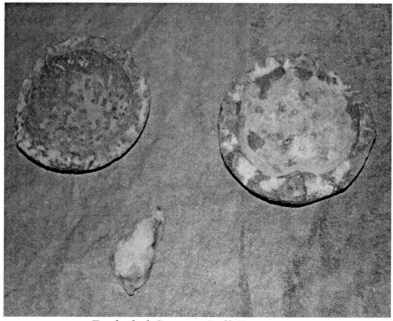

Exploded Cannon Ball Fragments

What is it? Unknown metal. The Size of cannon ball-Very Light Weight. Metal or Preserved Petrified Powder Load?

Left: 12 Pound solid Shot Cannon Ball

Right: Exploded Iron Cannon Ball Fragment that has Grape Shot of Various Sizes Displayed

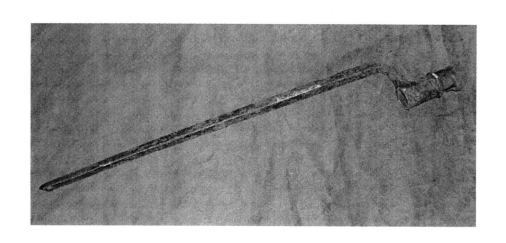

Triangular Blade Bayonets.

One complete and one that has been broken off.

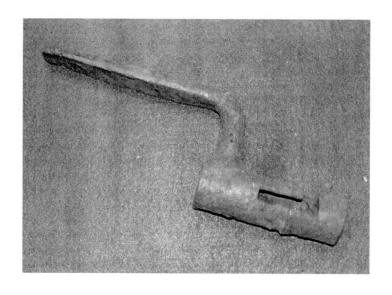

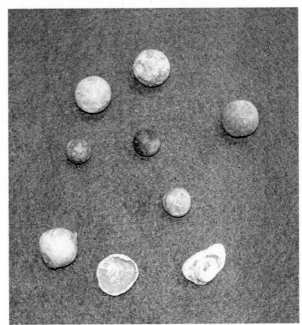

Above: Lead Case Shot. Some undamaged and 3 showing evidence of impact.

Below: Case Shot Mold – Used to make the style of shot shown above.

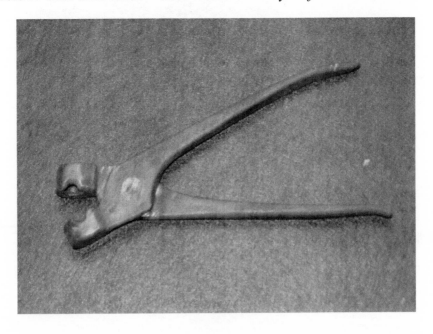

Above: Right is a Union Breastplate with what appears to be a bullet hole in it. The one on the left was not found at Natural Bridge but is shown so you can see what it looks like undamaged.

Below: Confederate breastplates-Very simple in design compared with that of the Union.

Percussion Cap Tin Cans

Metal Padlock or Lock Cover
Eagle Insignia Marked with
W.W. & Co
(Barnett, 2011)

Metal Horse Bridle Piece
Note Federal US marking
(Barnett, 2011)

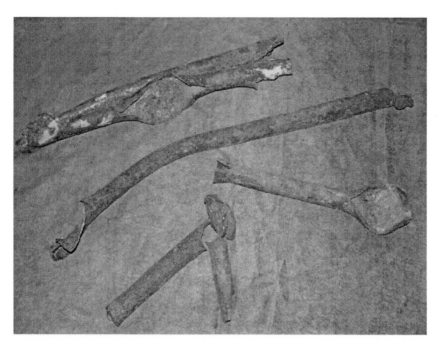

Above: Two shotgun barrels and two other pieces of gun barrels found together at the site.

Below: Two Stirrups

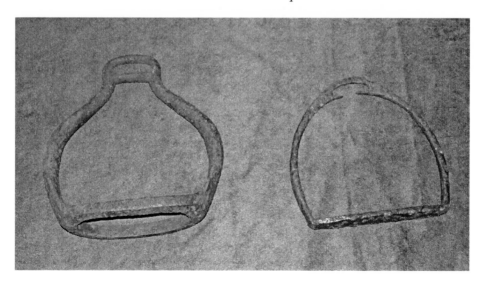

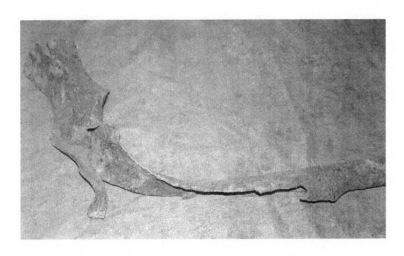

Above: shows one end that is completely split.

An exploded shot gun barrel that was found in a hole at the Burns Place along with several other damaged or blown apart barrels. The US Military had two regiments of black soldiers at Natural Bridge that were armed primarily with shot guns.

Below: shows entire barrel with damage to both ends.

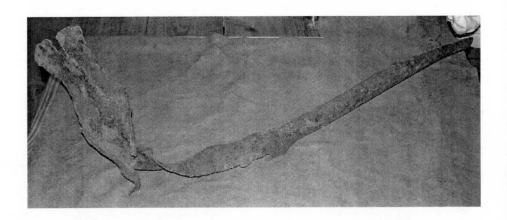

GLOSSARY

Chitlins - Hog Intestines or guts

Chitterlings - A more formal word for Hog Intestines or guts

Cracklin' bread - regular corn bread with the cracklin's cooked in with it

Cracklins - pork fat trimmings consisting of pieces with and without skin on them. These are cook or fried until all the lard is cooked out of them and you have pieces that are brown and crispy. These can be saved and use later.

Chufas - a bunch grass with a peanut like underground nut - used for food plots of deer, turkey, hogs and wild hogs. This legume is very similar to peanuts, if you have ever seen hogs rooting peanuts; they go after chufas the same way. Plant in spring through summer. Wildlife digs up the chufas once they mature.

Guano - bird manure, shipped in from South America and used as fertilizer

Hickor - Hickory Nuts

Holey Boley - A favorite treat. Take a biscuit and put a hole in it with your finger. Fill the hole with cane syrup and it is ready to eat.

Pummie pile – A pile of the crushed stalks of cane after they had gone through the mill.

BIBLIOGRAPHY

Allen R. Gerrell, J. (1993). *Kilcrease Light Artillery; 1863.* Tallahassee: Self Published.

Barnett, J. L. (2011, Spring). The Battle of Natural Bridge: The Private Collection of the Gerrell Family. *Thesis* . Tallahassee, FL.

Butler, M. G. (1996). *A Book of Halls.* Calvary, Georgia.

Crawford, H. C. (1914). Memoirs.

General Assembly of Florida, F. S. (Dec. 18, 1865). Acts & Resolutions. (p. Chapter 1518). Tallahassee: Offic of the Floridian: Printed by Dyke & Sparhawk.

Government, U. S. *1860 United Sates Federal Census record.*

Government, U. S. *1870 United Sates Federal Census Report.*

Smith, E. (1963, November). Magnolia Monthly.

the Sons of The Confederacy Camp Cresset #1614, F. B. (n.d.). Havana, Florida.

United States Government. (1910). *1910 United States Federal Census Record.*

INDEX

The Illustrated History of the Naval Stores (Turpentine Industry)

The book is a culmination of many years of enjoyable research by the author. The history of the turpentine industry was portrayed through the use of old photos, letters, advertisements, recipes and jokes. This illustrated history traces the industry from beginning to end in the 1970s.

PETE GERRELL was a sixth generation native of Florida. Generations of his family lived and survived in the pine flatwoods associated with the naval stores and timber industries. Throughout his life he collected information and artifacts having to do with these industries.

Copyright TXU 814-159 1997 by Pete Gerrell
ISBN 0-9665193-0-2
Library of Congress Catalog Card No. 98-90418

Southern Yellow Pine (SYP) Publishing
4351 Natural Bridge Rd
Tallahassee, FL 32305
www.syppublishing.com

The Heritage of Leon County, Florida; Historical Stories of Events, Places & People that Shaped Tallahassee

The Tallahassee Genealogical Society, Inc. has compiled a book that represents many of the threads that, over time, have been woven into the community of Leon County. The reader can find tales that describe Leon County as families learned to live in the wilds of northwest Florida, as well as, learn information about some family genealogies. Some tales chronicle the individual life of a unique person in the history of the county. You may read anecdotes about Grandma and how she shaped the lives of future generations or learn about renowned politicians. The reader can also discover information about some of the unique sites and landmarks in Leon County including Cascades Park and Mabry Field along with many other historical places and events of significance.

New Release

149

CPSIA information can be obtained at www.ICGtesting.com
Printed in the USA
LVOW100909041012

301295LV00002BA/2/P